Graham Kerr's

Gathering Place

Featuring

Nutrient-Rich
Comfort Food

The publisher gratefully acknowledges the support of the Government of Canada, Department of Canadian Heritage, Book Publishing Industry Development Program. Special thanks to Steve Thomson of Backstage Productions International.

ISBN 1-55082-274-8

Edited by Bob Hilderley.
Design by Susan Hannah.
Images captured by Round Table Productions.
Cover photograph by Ken Faught, The Toronto Star. Frontispiece photography by Peeps Photography.

Printed and bound by Everbest Canada.

Published by Quarry Press Inc., PO Box 1061, Kingston, Ontario K7L 4Y5 Canada
www.quarrypress.com.

VOLUME 1: Nutrient-Rich
          Entertainment Food
VOLUME 2: Nutrient-Rich
          Comfort Food
VOLUME 3: Nutrient-Rich
          Ethnic Food

Graham and Treena Kerr

Graham Kerr's  Gathering Place

"where the pan sizzles and science smiles"

Featuring Nutrient-Rich Comfort Food for Managing Weight,
Preventing Illness, and Creating a Happier Lifestyle

by Graham Kerr

QUARRY HEALTH BOOKS

$\mathcal{M}$enu

	Recipe	Nutrition Theme	Guest
	MAIN DISHES		
67	Steak and Oyster Pie	Nutrition and Disease Prevention	Ann Gallagher, RD Former President, American Dietetic Association
71	Meatloaf	The Psychology of Food	Paul Garfinkel, MD Chief of Psychiatry, University of Toronto
75	Three Sisters Stew	The Language of Flavor	Linda Bartoshuk, PhD Professor, Department of Surgery (Otolaryngology) and Psychology, Yale University
79	Cioppino	Celebrating the Family	David St. John-Grubb, MCFA (CG), CMC, CEC, CHE, MHCMA & Cathy Powers, MS, RD
83	Scottish Irish Stew	Food Portions	Lisa R. Young, MS, RD, CDN Doctoral Student, Nutrition and Food Studies, New York University
87	Cottage Pie	Tailored Cookbooks	Vic Strecher, MD, MPH Director and Professor, Health Media Research Labs, University of Michigan
91	Jerk Marinated Lamb Stew	Digestion Facts	Deanna L. Miller, RD Oropharyngeal Coordinator, Missouri Baptist Medical Center
95	Petite Coq au Vin	Fidget Factor	Victor L. Katch, PhD Professor, Kinesiology, University of Michigan
99	Yankee Pot Roast	Iron Clad Nutrition	Evelyn Tribole, MS, RD Author, *Stealth Health*
103	Pea Sea Pie	Farmers' Markets	Gail Feenstra, M.Ed., Ed.D. Food Systems Analyst, University of California, Davis
107	Seattle Summer Halibut	Feeding the Homeless	Cheryl Sesnon Former Executive Director, FareStart Program
111	St Augustine Perlow	Home Food Safety	Joan Horbiak, MPH, RD Former National Home Food Safety Spokesperson, American Dietetic Association
115	Chiliquiles	Snacking Successfully	Kathleen Zelman, MPH, RD Spokesperson, American Dietetic Association
119	Roast Chicken	Reliable Health Research	Rena A. Mendelson, D.Sc., MS Associate Vice-President Academic, Ryerson Polytechnic University
123	Boston Baked Beans	Exploring Folic Acid	Evelyn Tribole, MS, RD Author, *Stealth Health*
127	Jambalaya	African American Health Issues	Jeannette Jordan, MS, RD, CDE Prevention/Detection Education Coordinator, Medical University of South Carolina
131	Shrimp Gumbo	Gourmet-Style Hospital Food Service	Mary Kimbrough, RD, LD Director, Nutrition Services, Zale Lipshy University Hospital

Acknowledgements

As one advances in years (which is a better way to say 'getting older'), the list of those for whom one is truly grateful keeps getting longer . . .

My wife Treena remains my prime motivator. Suzanne Butler has been my senior food associate for nine years and counting. Chavanne Hanson has almost matched that record as the registered dietitian who offers nutritional knowledge and as the technical researcher / writer of the guests' comments. Wendall Wilkes was the Executive Producer of the television series, Steve Thomson the line producer, and Michael Carlisle my agent . . . without whose collective work I would have already retired.

Speaking of which . . . my personal secretary Karin Rowles has, in fact, retired. All of us miss her . . . dearly!

And especially Bob Hilderley and Susan Hannah who have husbanded this book so gracefully. Thank you all . . . I'm truly grateful.

Good Health in Good Taste
A Menu for a New Lifestyle

DURING THE 40 YEARS MY WIFE TREENA AND I have made television programs together and through the publication of over 14 million copies of our cookbooks, we have on occasion exceeded what we call the "speed-feed limit" while living the 'gourmet' lifestyle. In a word, we over-indulged and lived unreasonably. We simply ate more than our bodies were able to digest, consume, and combust. At one time during the 'Galloping Gourmet' era, we actually ate seven meals in one day in Paris, including meals at Tours d'Argent, The Ritz, and Hotel Meurice! Every dish was as delicious as it could possibly be . . . sauteed in clarified butter, often flamed in brandy, and drowned in cream. It made for good television, and the weight stayed off as long as we 'galloped' from meal to meal . . . well, almost.

Life eventually caught up to us and death came knocking at the door much too early in our lives. At age 53, Treena suffered a stroke, followed five months later by a heart attack, then the onset of diabetes. That year we began our journey together in search of wellness. We began a search to discover a way to live within reason at the end of what was for us an unreasonable age. We have always loved each other in the best and worst of times, and this love became a vital ingredient in our choice to change our lifestyle rather than swiftly submit to surgery and medication. Our cardiologist told us there was a window of opportunity for us to try prevention, perhaps even achieve a reversal, without the need for a heart bypass operation. Treena and I became more active, lost weight, ate in a completely different style. Thirteen years later we have greatly reduced her risk. We have literally won back our lives, day by day, eating well for good health.

Together we set out to learn more about human nutrition, inviting health-care professionals as guests on our new series of television shows, *Graham Kerr's Gathering Place*, where we use the knowledge shared by our guests to prepare nutritionally rich recipes for managing weight, preventing illness, and creating a happier lifestyle — all bursting with flavor. Each show features such a recipe, with the nutritional values of various foods discussed by our guests. At the end of each show, I serve the dish to my very professional guests as well as a member of the audience who gather around the 'home' dinner table on the set. To capture the immediacy of the preparation of the dish and my pleasure in the serving of the food to our guests, we have captured those moments in stills from the show.

Outside and Obvious

PART OF TREENA'S RETURN TO GOOD HEALTH and mine too (although I inherited great genes, my 'galloping' cholesterol was 265 mg per deciliter, while the normal total cholesterol is 200 mg per deciliter) has been due to gradual weight management. Over the years we gained weight because we became less active and ate more (especially portion size) while our overall metabolism changed with age. Since everyone's (well, almost everyone's) metabolism becomes less combustive with age and since this is gradual, it really does mean that a weight gain equals a change in eating or moving.

Just as weight gain does not simply happen, effective weight loss is a gradual process. When we set out to lose weight, we must do so for the long term. All of my guests on the television show agree that weight loss requires altering the basics by gradually eating a little less and moving a little more. But eat less of what and how to move ... and enjoy both eating and exercising . . . that is the 'outside and obvious' theme of many discussions in this book.

While this 'eat less and exercise more' axiom may seem simple to implement, weight management is complicated by attitude. A sudden need to lose 20 or 30 pounds for a wedding, class reunion, or vacation on the beach will attract rapid methods such as the various high protein, low carbohydrate 'diets', all having one factor in common — low calories, or eating less. While these fad diets sometimes work in the short run, when you return to 'whole' eating, the weight returns — and often more weight than when you started. To make weight loss long lasting and to avoid the health risks of unbalanced eating, you will need to follow the more conservative, gradual reduction suggestions made by my professional guests. Your job is to put their nutritional advice and my nutrient rich recipes to the test.

Here are seven personal observations and plans of action for successful weight management that we have discovered.

Reduce Fat: I learned that one gram of fat has 9 calories, while one gram of sweet potato (carbohydrate source) has 4 calories. Therefore, weight for weight, fat has over double the calories of carbohydrates. I've tried to reduce fats and increase carbohydrates in my diet.

Focus on the Complex (Carbohydrates): I prefer carbohydrates that come complete with a nutrient 'benefit package' — fiber, vitamins, antioxidants, and other phytochemicals that come *naturally* and have not been somehow manufactured, such as flour, bread, sugar, jams, cookies, pasta, polished rice, candy, etc. By no means do I banish *anything* — I simply choose to eat *less* manufactured/processed carbohydrates and *more* natural state carbohydrates, especially whole grains, beans, legumes (lentils, peas, etc.), and fresh vegetables and fruit.

Reduce the Refined: I began this choice by counting my consumption of manufactured and processed carbohydrates for a three-day period. It came to about 600 calories per day. I decided to halve the amount, thereby 'saving' 300 calories.

Add Activity: Restricting calories is only half the battle, so I added a deliberate *activity* (brisk walking for three miles and other flex/weight exercises). At my weight, this added up to 200 calories of effort.

Calories Reduced: I now had a daily deficit of 500 calories, which, since my weight had been more or less stable at 208 pounds, resulted in a slow but *reasonable* decline of about 3,500 calories per week. Interestingly, there are 3,500 calories in one pound of fat!

Muscles Increased: As I increased my aerobic activity from walking, combined with strength training, my muscles began to become denser, and since muscle weighs more than fat, I found that, on average, I lost about three pounds per month, rather than the four I would have expected. Over a four-month period, I was down to 195.5, losing over 12 pounds.

Look — no tears!

Freeze an onion for 15 minutes before chopping to decrease the volatile oils from spraying up and getting into your eyes.

Tracking Progress: I keep a daily journal for all kinds of reasons, one of which is to record my daily weight (yes, I do weigh myself *every single day* and so does Treena). 'Isn't that obsessive/compulsive behavior?' you might ask. I'm inclined to think not, largely because we live in a minefield of temptation and need to be very careful where we put our feet (so to speak). We travel with a small Healthometer digital scale which is essential for helping us stay 'on track' away from home.

I transfer Treena's weight to a separate graph that also tracks her blood sugar and blood pressure. We call it 'The Daily Olympics of Life'. We are literally in a training mode for wellness. We know what it's like to be sick and we know what it's like to exceed the speed-feed limit. This simple daily discipline has helped us avoid both. It also allows us to work with great confidence to develop better and better tastes, aromas, colors, and textures in what has become, for us, a comforting, safe environment.

The process was slow enough so as not to seem like a diet, and I've made these choices the foundation of a new healthier and happier lifestyle, so, in a *real* sense, gradual weight loss has worked for me. Treena has applied the same ideas to achieve an eight-pound loss.

Inside & Hidden

YOU CAN'T SEE IT, OFTEN YOU CAN'T FEEL IT . . . until it bites you! While extra weight is outside and obvious, we have found that related health problems, like the dirty duo of diabetes and hypertension, are *almost* invisible. And *there's* the problem. How to wrestle with something serious when it doesn't hurt and remains, for most of its development, hidden? This is where measurement is vital. My good friend Julia Child once said, 'you can eat anything if you eat it in moderation.' I agreed, yet added, 'providing you know what is, for *you*, moderate — and that needs *measurement.*'

Dr Castelli, Director of the Framingham Heart Study, says that most folks tell him, 'Why look under the hood if it's going good?' In our case, Treena started out with a stroke *before* we found out about her 365 mg/dL cholesterol level (normal is 200 mg/dcL), hypertension, and diabetes. Surely, that's the wrong way round. When once we discovered her numbers and were told what would be 'good' to aim for, we developed a 'frame' for living, rather like a picture frame. After all, if you want to be a picture of health, why not live within reasonable limits? When we live within the frame, *we live within reason.* When we step out beyond the frame is when the choice becomes *unreasonable.*

Here is the big picture of some of the choices we've made. You might begin now to frame your life so as to *prevent* illness rather than recover from it, as we did.

1. Choose to eat less fat (especially saturated fats) and *fewer* manufactured carbohydrates. Don't necessarily ban cookies and pastries, but keep portions limited. Skip bread and butter before a meal. Enjoy eggs but limit eggs to one or two times a week.

2. Eat *lots more* fresh fruits and vegetables that provide phytochemicals, fiber, and other nutrients to your daily diet. You may go ahead and supplement your diet with vitamins and minerals, but do not use supplements as a substitute for good food. There are so many substances found in fruits and vegetables that are not found in supplements.

3. Select quite small portions of animal protein. Four ounces a day should be quite enough. Enjoy eggs but limit eggs to one or two times a week. Be careful *not* to substitute meat for vegetables (high protein diets). This may seem to work for quick weight loss, but it's not wise in the long term for good health — which is our goal, after all.

4. When you eat in a restaurant, plan ahead and think through what you will order before you go. Keep meat portions limited to three-ounce portions by splitting an entrée, if nec-

essary, and ask for additional vegetables. Skip bread and butter before a meal. Finger foods at cocktail parties can add up, so before you go have a small bowl of soup or a half sandwich to take the edge off your appetite. It will be much easier to skip the cheese, crackers and hors d'oeuvres that so quickly add up in fat and calories.

5. Face your challenges head on. Chocolate was a downfall for me until I eliminated it totally from my diet for 10 months. By then the behavior change was *transparent* and a regular part of my life. When I tried chocolate again, I felt in control and limited my portion significantly and without any difficulty.

6. As for beverages, limit alcohol to no more than two glasses of wine a day. Try de-alchoholized wines. And drink lots of water — 6-8 eight-ounce glasses each day.

7. If you smoke, stop to reduce your health risks significantly.

If you want to be a picture of health, why not live within reasonable limits? When we live within the frame, we live within reason. When we step out beyond the frame, the choice becomes unreasonable.

8. Know your numbers *now*. Weigh yourself. Test your blood pressure. Have a fasting (12 hour) blood lipid test and record your present numbers:
   Total Cholesterol
   HDL Cholesterol
   LDL Cholesterol
   Triglycerides (blood fats)
   Blood Glucose
   Glycated Hemoglobin (Hba1c)
In consultation with a health care professional, set numbers you can *realistically* use as a future goal.
   Take a look at how the choices we made had an impact on our health:

Treena's Test Results	Before	After	Normal
Weight	154 lbs	130 lbs	Varies
Blood Pressure	160/87	145/75	under 140/80
Total Cholesterol	365 mg/dL	145 mg/dcL	under 200 mg/dL
LDL Cholesterol	163 mg/dL	83 mg/dL	under 100 mg/dL
Blood Glucose	165 mg/dL	130 mg/dL	under 110 mg/dL
Glycated Hemoglobin	11.0%	6.5%	4-6%

Since we intended to start a 'reasonable' exercise/fitness program we also wanted to have a way to gauge our progress. We wanted to know our percentage of body fat, our resting metabolic rate, and the rate of oxygen uptake by lean muscle tissue, using a treadmill test.

Graham's Test Results:

Bioelectrical Impedance Analysis/Body Fat Percentage Measurement:
27% (about 5-7% higher than 'reasonable' for my age)

Resting Metabolic Rate:
1740 calories for 24 hours (use this as a place to start for your calorie needs, but you may need to increase this number as you have varying levels of activity reach day)

Oxygen Uptake/Treadmill Test:
22 milliliters per kilogram registered (normal)

All in all I have got room for 'measurable' improvement, a goal to reach by next year, which is a motive for the best of intentions!

If you want to find your specific measurements, may I suggest that you visit with your personal physician who can place you in contact with a nearby university, hospital, or health clinic that can perform these assessments. If so, maybe they could include you in their research numbers — you may just strike it lucky, as I did! Failing that, there are a few modern devices often found at fitness centers that can produce a set of fairly accurate numbers to use as a yardstick for personal achievement.

Remember, your aim here is to make good food the agent of good, not bad, health.

Hoffen and Away

THE GERMAN PEOPLE HAVE A tremendous word they love to use to express a special emotional and spiritual experience. 'Hoffen' means 'to leap up *inside* with expectation.' It's where we get the word hope, but the word also involves *big time encouragement*. In my search for wellness, I keep looking for the hoffen-ings, ideas that get you up on your feet yelling, 'YES — I CAN DO THAT!' However, I've never let a one-liner be the sole guide to a decision. If I feel the *hoffen*, then I set out to educate myself full bore on the subject. When I know why something works, then I'm much more disciplined in its practice.

For example, Dr James Prochaska's famous 'Five Stages of Behavior Change' has had a profound effect upon my life, even to the extent that Treena and I have renamed some of the stages of change we have experienced in our own relationship and relationships with others. We had been preoccupied with ourselves, then began to look outward following our own 'C5' program.

- C1: Concern (for our own well-being)
- C2: Consideration (for the well-being of others)
- C3: Commitment (to change)
- C4: Create (new ways of living)
- C5: Communicate (our enthusiasm)

Hoffen means 'to leap up inside with expectation.'

"We need to make changes that are truly liveable," Dr Jeff Janata observes. "We need to be strategic about the changes we make and make sure we make them in ways that are transparent so they don't feel like a burden to us."

And so the change in eating 'style' we recommend in this book should likewise not feel like a burden. There is absolutely no need for taste and pleasure to suffer because our food choices and food preparation are healthy. Our diet can be nutrient rich and delicious. Within this book are literally hundreds of hoffen-ings from really well-informed doctors, scientists, registered dietitians, and chefs. By all means, let their *hoffens* be the spark that ignites your desire to make a change in your lifestyle!

Nutrient Rich Recipes

WE MUST LOOK FOR FOOD that gives us as much 'bang for our buck' as possible to manage weight, prevent illness, and lift our spirit. To determine these foods, we have developed a formula we call T.A.C.T. x N.D.F. For fruits and vegetables, we drew up this brief T.A.C.T. chart as an example:

Taste   salt (celery), sweet (honeydew melon), sour (lemon), bitter (radiccio)
Aroma   basil, gingerroot, garlic
Color   peppers, radish, tomatoes, black olives, spinach
Texture   hot peppers, banana, cucumber

Draw up your own chart and keep adding to it as you explore more T.A.C.T. 'full' foods.

Then we analyzed our meals for Nutrient Dense Foods (N.D.F.), measuring total calories, fat (unsaturated and saturated), percentage calories from fat, carbohydrates, fiber, and sodium content. We could likewise analyze them for their vitamin and mineral values. Then in presenting each recipe, we created a 'Nutritional Profile' comparing a new nutrient-rich version with an old-style, 'galloping' version. Here's what the 'Nutritional Profile' looks like for an old Kerr family breakfast favorite, 'Kerr Mush' (a somewhat 'un'-flattering name for oatmeal porridge).

In presenting each recipe, we created a 'Nutritional Profile' comparing a new nutrient-rich version with an old-style, 'galloping' version.

Nutritional Profile (Kerr Mush)

Per Serving	Nutrient Rich	Old Style
calories	255	188
fat (g)	6	8
saturated fat (g)	1	4
carbohydrates(g)	42	23
fiber (g)	3	2
sodium (mg)	87	663

We've reduced fat, increased carbohydrates and fiber, while cutting sodium over seven fold — all without reducing taste, aroma, color, or texture. Indeed, we've often improved T.A.C.T. when we've used N.D.F. foods.

Taste, Aroma, Color, Texture multiplied by Nutrient Dense Foods replaces a millennium-old culinary habit of using excessive amounts of refined starches and sugar, animals fats and proteins to create flavor while meeting our nutritional needs.

Live Food

PREPARING FOOD FOR PRESENTATION on television and in books has always been a somewhat artificial process. Dishes being cooked on the set are often replaced by a finished version prepared hours before so everything looks 'just right'. Colors are enhanced with food coloring, special lights are focused on the food, bright raw vegetables replace bland cooked ones, and a whole host of chemical substances are applied to preserve, prop, and primp the dish for film reproduction. While this 'super-styled' food may look appetizing, it is inedible — and unattainable for the home cook who hopes to make the dish look like the picture on the screen or in the book.

On *Graham Kerr's Gathering Place*, however, we have presented the food 'live'. Once I have prepared the dish, I serve it to our special guest and to a member of the audience who joins us at the table. No special effects, no props, just the 'styling' I can give when arranging the food on the plates or in the bowls, often served under a certain amount of duress. Without the pressure of a live audience watching your every move, your home version of each dish may even look better than mine. In this book, we have tried to capture this 'live' feel by reproducing digital images of each meal in motion, either as I am cooking the food or serving the meal to my guests. To know that the food in this book is live and edible is comforting in itself.

"It must have been something I 'eight'!"

A Gathering Place

I PASSIONATELY BELIEVE that the home dining table is our last remaining tribal gathering place. Sitting face-to-face, elbow-to-elbow over hot, steaming plates of simple comfort food, we nourish our bodies and feed our souls. This is the place where families and friends gather, communities take shape, and hospitality beckons, where self-worth is fostered. And finally, a place where tender feelings and ruffled feathers can be soothed simply by breaking bread together. But images of gourmet meals have placed the emphasis on the presentation of complex recipes, not the pleasure and value of eating simple foods. Now I'm devoted to finding creative, healthy ways to bring us all back to the table. There are no strict rules at The Gathering Place table, no absolutely good or absolutely bad foods, only a tempting array of creative choices that can help you and your family celebrate being alive and well one day after another. This volume of *Graham Kerr's Gathering Place* features comfort foods, recipes that warm the heart. And while classic comfort foods, often rich in fats and sugar, are not usually associated with good health, these recipes are most certainly nutritious.

Dinner gatherings are also a wonderful way of enjoying an evening with friends and exploring just how delicious good nutritious food can taste. We have dinners for six where our guests do two-thirds of the work. They provide the appetizer and dessert while we do the main dish. We try to place the food into a frame of less than 1,000 calories with only 20% or less of those calories from fat. With the world of food out there, it's a wonderfully creative set of choices and great fun to delight each other without doing any harm. We also set an empty place for a 'seventh guest' that we designate to the homeless, victims of fire or flood, or the ill — someone who, for all kinds of reasons, cannot make it to the table. We later send funds to a trusted agency that can provide our 'seventh guest' with a healthy meal.

My goal with *The Gathering Place* television series and cookbooks is to inspire you to make family gatherings part of your life again, but with a few twists. I am convinced that we entertain our friends and nourish our families even better by using fresh, whole foods with exciting flavors without the excessive use of fat, sugar, or salt. Together we can create a menu for a better lifestyle eating good food in good taste. We can live life to the fullest with energy to spare for those in need of special care.

Grandma Yan's Porridge & 'Kerr' Mush

When I invited Martin Yan to appear on my show as a guest chef, little did I know that we would end up having a 'cook off' with Martin preparing a nutritious and flavorful Chinese porridge based on his grandmother's recipe, while I prepared a high fiber, low fat, low sodium version of our favorite family comfort breakfast, Kerr Mush. Often overlooked in cookbooks — and all too often neglected in our 'gulp-n-go' world — breakfast can be fun!

The Chinese give us a unique opportunity to see how to do things right! This wonderful culture eats a high carbohydrate diet with lots of noodles, rice, and vegetables for sustenance and nutrition, a touch of meat for flavoring and protein, and a true focus on down-to-earth comfort foods, family favorites, where nothing is fancy, but instead always seasonal and nutritional. Here's Martin Yan's grandmother's recipe for porridge.

Breakfast & Brunch

Ingredients:

Grandma Yan's Porridge

1 1/2 cups uncooked long-grain rice
1 tablespoon shredded ginger
12 cups chicken broth
1/2 pound boneless chicken,
   cut into small pieces

Marinade

2 teaspoons cornstarch
1/4 teaspoon salt
1/8 teaspoon white pepper
1 teaspoon sesame oil

Garnishes

Chopped cilantro
Thinly sliced green onion
Roasted peanuts

Ingredients:

Kerr Mush

1 1/4 cups rolled oats
1/4 cup dark raisins and cranberries mixed
2 2/3 cups nonfat milk
2 teaspoons brown sugar
   (or 2 packets of 'Splenda')
1/4 cup Graham's Seed and Nut Mix:
   Combine equal measures of sunflower
   seeds, unhulled sesame seeds, green
   pumpkin seeds, sliced almonds, and a half
   measure of ground flax seeds. Make a big
   batch and keep it tightly covered in the
   refrigerator for handy use.

Grandma Yan's Porridge

1. In a large pot, combine rice, ginger, and broth; bring to a boil. Reduce heat, cover, and simmer, stirring occasionally, until rice becomes very soft and creamy, about 1 1/2 hours.
2. While rice is cooking, combine marinade ingredients in a bowl; add chicken and stir to coat
3. Add chicken to pot and simmer, stirring occasionally, for 10 minutes. Stir in sesame oil.
4. To serve, ladle porridge into individual soup bowls and top with garnishes.

Makes 6-8 servings.

(Copyright by Yan Can Cook, Inc. 1999)

Kerr Mush

Well now, here it is, our winter breakfast six days a week! The Kerr family porridge, revised to boost fiber and lower fats and sodium. How do we put up with this lack of variety? Simple ... it's fantastic (and I am Scottish). The low temperature soak 'n' heat method looks odd, but it gives you time to shower and dress. This is so simple and so fool-proof that it makes eating a nutritious breakfast possible everyday (especially if you are Scottish).

1. Simmer the oats, raisins, and milk over low heat, covered, until warmed through and plump (15-20 minutes . . . while you shower and dress).

2. When thoroughly warmed, raise the heat to medium and stir vigorously until it goes creamy-thick in texture, less than one minute.

3. Add 1/4 of the seed and nut mix and serve with a 'dusting' of brown sugar. Better not leave the sugar bowl within reach — more than 1 teaspoon is really unnecessary! Recently we have begun to season our 'mush' with a Sri Lankan Sweet Spice, 1/4 teaspoon per plate. To find this recipe, see ETHMIX on my website, www.grahamkerr.com

Serves 2

Classic Chinese Comfort Cooking

The herbal medicine shops of Hong Kong and Chinatowns around the world are renowned for their vast selections of hard-to-find herbal remedies. The most popular shops are the ones with a full-time doctor on staff to consult with customers and write prescriptions. There's always a musty but not unpleasant odor in these shops — something like a cross between wet earth, tea, and lemons. The walls are lined with cabinets and jars containing an unending array of powder, berries, roots, and more. Chefs and savvy cooks like Martin Yan know that these shops are also the best places to find all kinds of premium dried ingredients and seasonings for cooking. Chinese cooking is quick, fun, flavorful, and healthy.

Martin Yan, CMC, MS
Television Host, *Yan Can Cook, So Can You!*
Author, *Yan Can Cook, Martin Yan's Feast, The Best of Yan Can Cook,* and *Chinese Cooking for Dummies*

What are the primary elements of classic Chinese cooking?

The basic flavor profile is simple yet profound and you can create almost anything with these flavorings:

* ginger
* garlic
* green onion
* soy sauce
* sesame oil
* oyster sauce
* hoisin (plum based sauce)
* rice vinegar
* five spice powder

But the most important kitchen tool is a knife-styled cleaver, particularly for Asian cuisine. (*And we all know how adept Martin is with his knife.*)

What are current health and food trends of the Chinese people?

The Chinese these days are more stressed than in the past and their diet is changing because of the growing contact with the Western world, but overall there is less sugar, cream, and butter in the diet than in North America and Europe. Very few Chinese are overweight. In the

NUTRITIONAL PROFILE COMPARISON (KERR MUSH)

Per serving	Nutrient Rich	Old Style
calories	255	188
fat (g)	6	8
saturated fat (g)	1	4
carbohydrates (g)	42	23
fiber (g)	3	2
sodium (mg)	87	663

north, the typical menu is predominately noodle dishes, while in the south rice dishes are most common. These dishes feature lots of vegetables, many are vegetarian, with meat and shellfish used as flavoring along with herbs and spices. Fresh fruit is dessert — and the people are healthy as a result.

For more information contact: http//www.yancancook.com

*B*reakfast Tacos with Refried Beans

San Antonio, Texas

*F*or breakfast aim to include foods rich in calcium as well as fiber for optimal nutrition at the beginning of the day. Start the day nutrient rich. Fruits and vegetables are ideal, including the avocado and pinto beans featured in Mexican breakfast cuisine. Eggs for protein are good, too — but don't overdo this popular breakfast food. Consider using cholesterol-free, low-fat egg substitutes.

We have a great local restaurant that serves a truly memorable Huevos Rancheros for breakfast. We also live in an area that hosts numerous Mexican farm workers during the harvest season — and they are not going to be fooled by an imitation! However, that doesn't mean that there is no room for innovation. In San Antonio, for example, there are all kinds of breakfast 'tacos' using both traditional and contemporary ideas, like this very pleasant 'omelet' presented on refried beans with a very different guacamole. Well worth a try, it makes a great weekend brunch dish, but probably won't fool any visiting rancheros!

Breakfast & Brunch

Ingredients:

Yogurt Guacamole
1 Haas avocado
1 tablespoon freshly squeezed lime juice
1/4 cup yogurt cheese (see 'The Basics')
1/4 teaspoon salt
pinch cayenne pepper

Refried Beans
1/2 teaspoon non-aromatic olive oil
1/4 cup finely chopped onion
1 clove garlic, bashed and chopped
1 cup cooked pinto beans or nonfat canned
　refried beans
1 cup bean cooking liquid or water

Eggs
2 cups egg substitute
1 tablespoon finely diced reconstituted
　ancho chile (soak in hot water to
　reconstitute)
4-ounces (113 gm) finely diced Canadian
　bacon
1/4 cup thinly sliced green onions
1/8 teaspoon salt

4 warm flour tortillas

Breakfast Tacos with Refried Beans

1. Cut the avocado around the middle to remove the large central pit and spoon out the flesh. Mash the avocado with a fork. Add the lime juice, yogurt cheese, salt, and cayenne. Cover closely with plastic wrap and set aside.

2. Heat the oil in a skillet on medium high. Sauté the onions until tender, then add garlic and cook 30 seconds longer. Add the beans, mashing while you fry them. Pour in cooking liquid, as you need it. When a nice brown crust forms on the bottom of the pan, push it into the beans giving them more and more flavor as you continue to cook them. When they are dark and flavorful and a good spreading consistency, set aside and cover to keep warm.

3. Spread refried beans on each warm tortilla. Heat a small nonstick omelet pan on medium. Spray with pan spray and pour in 1/2 cup of the egg substitute. Push in the sides of the omelet as it cooks to a soft, still wet looking texture. Sprinkle with 1/4 of the diced chile, Canadian bacon, green onion, and a little salt. Lift and lay on a bean-covered tortilla. Repeat with the other three. Top with a dollop of yogurt guacamole and some chopped cilantro.

Serves 4

Special Techniques:

* Freeze an onion for 15 minutes before chopping to decrease the volatile oils from spraying up and getting into your eyes.

A Key to a Healthier Day

When I asked registered dietitian Cecelia Fileti to discuss on our show the wealth of opportunities each of us has to make breakfast nutritious, she provided more knowledge than I had bargained for. I have sometimes looked at mealtimes as an oasis, a place of peace, calm, respite, recovery, restoration . . . a time to reflect, even build a personal relationship, 40 minutes at least. But the breakfast oasis is often just a mirage for most people. Cecelia stresses the fundamental role of this meal in creating good health and keeping our spirits high throughout the day.

What is the importance of a good breakfast for human nutrition?

Cecilia Fileti, MS, RD, FADA
President, C.P. Fileti Associates, Inc

* Evidence shows that breakfast is a key to a healthier day because food in the morning serves to feed our bodies and our minds. Balanced breakfast meals can help our energy level, our competitive performance, and our eating and snacking habits later in the day, especially the problem of satiety, feeling 'full', rather than finding ourselves ravenous before lunch.
* The effect of a nutritious breakfast on children's health and behavior is very clear. Children who eat a good breakfast have a better attention span, enhanced cognition, and better school attendance records. They are less tardy — and have fewer visits to the nurse.

What tips do you have for making breakfast nutritious?

* Increase calcium with fruit smoothies and packaged cereals with milk.
* Increase fiber (20-35 grams a day is recommended by The National Cancer Institute), with whole grain cereals and breads and fruit.
* Increase fresh fruit, which can be very nutritious and quick.
* Add flax seed to recipes and on top of cereals.
* Monitor portion sizes in order to control calories.

NUTRITIONAL PROFILE COMPARISON

Per serving	Nutrient Rich	Old Style
calories	341	458
fat (g)	9	28
saturated fat (g)	2	10
carbohydrates (g)	37	32
fiber (g)	6	7
sodium (mg)	820	825

Breakfast that has a good balance of carbohydrates, protein, and a small amount of fat will sustain and energize a person during the whole morning, preventing us from getting ravenous. Research shows that nutrients are not made up if you skip breakfast, even if your first meal is later, so make sure you choose nutrient dense foods early in the morning.

Do different lifestyles require different approaches to eating breakfast?

Gulp-N-Go: A fiber bar or cereal bar might be a quick and easy alternative as a meal replacement, but beware of the fat and sugar content of these breakfast bars.

Mouse Potato: While sitting at your computer, have a small bowl of dried fruit along with a fruit smoothie for nutrient dense choices.

Road Warriors: Pack a breakfast on your way out the door to the car, plane, or train — a sandwich and a piece of fruit are great for supplying important nutrients while you are on the run.

For further information on this topic contact: www.eatright.org. There is also a wonderful manual that people can download on their computer called, *It's All About You . . . Making Healthy Choices,* at www.ificinfo.health.org.

$\mathcal{E}$ggs Ottawa

Ottawa, Ontario

$\mathcal{Y}$ou may have heard the term 'good' cholesterol and 'bad' cholesterol used when 'heart health' is being discussed and wondered if there is a simple explanation for the difference. Well, let's see! 'Good' or _Helpful refers to HDL, high-density lipoproteins which have the unique ability to dislodge cholesterol from artery walls and deposit it in the liver to be excreted from the body. "Bad' or _Lousy refers to LDL, low density lipoproteins which generally end up clogging arteries and wreaking havoc on your health. Simply remember to strive for High levels of the HDL and Low levels of LDL!

I have very warm feelings for the city of Ottawa. It was there, in 1968, that we began the Galloping Gourmet television series. No matter what the weather, our faithful audiences turned out every night and filled every seat. I needed to develop one dish and name it for Ottawa, just as a small way of saying 'thank you'. This is my take on the Eggs Benedict original created for Mr & Mrs LeGrand Benedict at Delmonico's Hotel in New York . . . but with over ten times less saturated fat than in the old style. If you serve fruit first and another muffin after, it makes a great brunch dish at only 400 calories!

Breakfast & Brunch

Ingredients:

1 teaspoon non-aromatic olive oil
4 jumbo mushroom caps (2 1/2", 6.5 cm),
  stems removed
2 teaspoons lemon juice
1/2 teaspoon dill weed
1/8 teaspoon ground cayenne pepper
1 teaspoon light butter flavored margarine
1 1/2 cups egg substitute
2 English muffins, split and toasted
4 slices (1 oz, 28 g each) Canadian bacon
8 slices (1 oz, 28 g each) low-fat
  mozzarella cheese
1 tablespoon finely chopped green onions

Eggs Ottawa

1. Heat the oil in a chef's pan on medium high. Set the mushroom caps in the hot pan stem side up. Pour 1/2 teaspoon of the lemon juice in each one and season with dill weed and cayenne pepper. Cook 6 minutes or until the lemon juice starts to steam. Turn and cook 1 more minute. Remove to a warm plate and cover.

2. Wipe out the pan and melt the margarine on medium high. Pour in the egg substitute and let it start to cook on the bottom without stirring. Egg substitute needs to be handled gently. Slowly push the cooked part of the egg to the center of the pan with a flat ended spurtle or spatula. When it's ready, it will still be slightly runny on the top. Please don't over cook it!

3. Preheat the broiler. Place the toasted muffin halves on the rack on a broiler pan. Lay the Canadian bacon on the muffin. Cover each muffin with 1/4 of the cooked eggs, press down firmly to make an even mound. Set the cooked mushrooms, stem side down, on top of the eggs and push down so the egg goes up into the cavity. Top with 2 slices overlapping of mozzarella. Place under the broiler 1 1/2 minutes or until the cheese is melted and begins to brown. Sprinkle with green onions and serve.

Serves 4

Special Techniques:

* Roll a lemon before you juice it so that you can break up the lemon in the center and extract more juice.
* If you cannot find egg substitutes, simply use egg whites (2 egg whites = 1 egg = 1/4 cup egg substitute). Although it lacks the golden color, egg substitute is essentially the same food.

Reversing Heart Disease

When cardiologist John Schroeder visited The Gathering Place we discussed heart disease, a subject close to the 'heart' of at least the 50% of us who are at risk. Dr Schroeder looked closely at the dietary causes of heart disease, especially arterial problems, isolating the major dietary culprit as saturated fats that often have an impact on our (Lousy)LDL cholesterol. Take heart — even the desserts we've created reduce saturated fats to the minimum without sacrificing flavor or aroma! By changing our lifestyle, reversing heart disease is possible.

What causes heart disease?

* Heart disease is caused by the things you do to injure the small coronary arteries that feed blood to your heart. Smoking, high blood pressure, a sedentary lifestyle, and diabetes are considered primary risk factors — as well as a diet high in saturated fats and LDL cholesterol.
* LDL cholesterol damages arteries by clogging them and thus impeding blood flow. Depending upon your genes and the food you consume, the more often and more intensely your arteries can become clogged.
* The foods that have the greatest impact on our LDL are saturated fats — dairy and meat fats as well as many baked goods that are processed with saturated fat like lard.

What steps can we take to avoid damage to our artery walls?

1. Reduce Saturated Fats: limit to 15-20 grams per day, though the average person eats 50-75 grams per day. If you eat 25 grams a day or less, you can dramatically reduce your cholesterol count and may even begin to reverse heart disease. You should work with a registered dietitian or other health care professional to help you achieve this goal.
2. Exercise: Begin a walking program or some form of exercise that gets you moving, but before you begin consult with your doctor.
3. Stop Smoking: If you smoke, stop immediately.

John Schroeder, MD
Professor, Cardiovascular Medicine, Stanford University
Co-Author, *The Stanford University Healthy Heart Cookbook & Life Plan*

NUTRITIONAL PROFILE COMPARISON

Per serving	Nutrient Rich	Old Style
calories	252	865
fat (g)	7	69
saturated fat (g)	3	37
carbohydrates (g)	29	29
fiber (g)	0	0
sodium (mg)	131	1949

What are the current medical treatments for coronary artery disease?

Besides heart surgery or angioplasty, statin drugs can reduce risk of dying or having a second event by 50%. This should be coupled with appropriate lifestyle changes and should be prescribed by a physician.

What else can we do to reverse heart disease?

* Check your family medical records for a history of diabetes. Stay thin and exercise, which can delay or prevent disease. Blood sugars should be checked every year and there are wonderful medicines that can help if you do have diabetes.
* Keep total cholesterol under 200 mg/dl and LDL cholesterol less than 100 mg/dl. If you cannot do it with lifestyle alone, medicine, with a physician's recommendation, may be of great help. If you already have heart disease, diabetes, or high blood pressure (major risk factors), a cholesterol value of 180mg/dl or even lower may be indicated.

For further information on this topic contact: http://cvmed.stanford.edu/default.htm or http://www.stanfordlifeplan.com/ or read John Schroeder's book, *The Stanford University Healthy Heart Cookbook & Life Plan.*

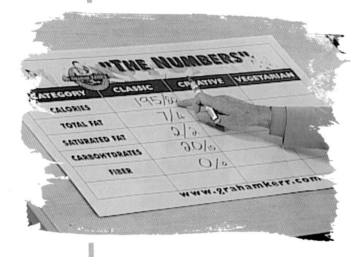

*B*lake Island Skillet Soufflé

Seattle, Washington

*R*ecently a whole slew of low carbohydrate, high protein 'diets' have claimed our attention, again. But the fat in animal protein, such as eggs, bacon, steaks, chops, and poultry, can contribute to increased 'bad' cholesterol, which may result in heart disease or some cancers. Remember, all fat has over double the calorie value of the same measure of carbohydrates — and calories will always be the deciding factor in long-lasting weight loss.

The restaurant is called Tillicum Village (that's the main attraction on the small Blake Island, a short boat ride from Seattle's fabulous waterfront). Tillicum sets out to give you an upscale glimpse at what life was like before the white man arrived. The food is all very well done, especially the salmon . . . split and roasted around an alder fire until fragrantly perfect! There was no point in me trying to reproduce the method, so I decided to use the readily available salmon lox (the salmon for which bagels and cream cheese were invented!) and produce an island of an omelet, cooked in a skillet. It's my gift to those who work so well to capture the original art forms of the Pacific Northwest.

Breakfast & Brunch

Ingredients:

¹/₄ cup sun dried tomatoes
2 green onions
4-ounces (114 g) salmon lox
¹/₂ teaspoon non-aromatic olive oil
¹/₂ cup 2% milk
1 tablespoon cornstarch
pinch nutmeg
pinch saffron
¹/₄ teaspoon freshly ground
  black pepper
1 egg yolk
1 teaspoon chopped fresh tarragon
  or ¹/₄ teaspoon dried
4 large egg whites
¹/₄ teaspoon cream of tartar
1 teaspoon butter
1 tablespoon parmesan cheese
1 tablespoon chopped parsley

Blake Island Skillet Soufflé

1. Bring 1 cup water to a boil in a small saucepan, add the sun dried tomatoes, reduce the heat and simmer 15 minutes. Drain and chop. Slice the green onions and set aside. Lay the slices of lox on top of each other and cut into ¹/₂" (1.5 cm) pieces.
2. Heat the oil in a saucepan on medium high. Sauté the onions 1 minute to release the flavors and add the tomatoes. Combine the milk, cornstarch, nutmeg, saffron and pepper and add to the onion mixture. Stir until thick, 30 seconds, then remove from the heat to cool. Mix in the egg yolk and tarragon and set aside.
3. Preheat the oven broiler. Beat the egg whites until foamy. Add the cream of tartar and continue beating until stiff peaks form. Stir ¹/₃ of the whites into the flavor base to lighten, then fold in the rest gently.
4. Melt the butter in a hot 10-inch omelet pan and allow it to brown slightly. Pour in the egg white mixture, stir quickly, then smooth and cook 30 seconds on medium high. Scatter the salmon evenly over the top and sprinkle with the cheese. Cook under the preheated broiler 3 to 4 minutes or until puffed and golden. Garnish with the parsley. Take the hot pan to the table, cut into fourths and serve on 4 hot plates. Served with an attractive salad, this can make a wonderfully tasty light brunch or supper dish.

Serves 4 for a brunch or light supper or 2 for a normal meal or 1 if you're *really* hungry!

Vegetarian Option: Blake Island Skillet Soufflé

You can make this dish vegetarian by replacing the salmon lox with 1/2 cup bright red, roasted sweet red peppers, cut in strips and 2 tablespoons capers.

Exploring Protein

Protein is utilized in the body to build and repair body tissues, hormones, enzymes, hair, and skin. Protein helps to keep the heart beating. Basically, every bodily function relies on protein. It is essential to life. So, we need protein, but how much and from what sources? Will eating lots of protein result in long-lasting weight loss? Or excessively large muscles? These are some of the questions Professor Jacqueline Berning addressed when she appeared as a guest on our show.

What are common sources of dietary protein?

Protein is found in both animals and plants, including, nuts, beans, soy protein, chicken, fish, cheese and dairy products, egg whites, and meat. Protein is constructed of amino acids: there are 22 amino acids in total, nine of which are essential and must be consumed through the diet. Foods containing all essential amino acids, primarily animal sources, are considered complete proteins. Plant proteins contain some of the amino acids but may be missing one or more, and are considered incomplete proteins. When you combine two plant proteins together, like rice and beans, you can get all the amino acids to make a complete protein. This does not have to happen at the same meal, it just needs to be in the same day.

What happens if you have too much protein?

A great deal of stress is placed on the kidneys and ketones and toxins build up in the body, which must be eliminated in order to maintain good health. The stress placed on the body results in the tearing down of muscle tissue. Muscles come from weight training and not from the amount protein consumed.

What happens if you have too little protein?

The body will break down its own muscle mass in order to acquire the amino acids it needs.

And when you diet?

If you don't put any food in your body, you will use your own muscle tissue as the fuel source. Lean body mass heads out the door and fat is left on the body. Water and lean muscle mass will be lost, and you will see this loss at a very rapid rate (5–8 pounds in one week).

Jacqueline Berning, PhD, RD
Assistant Professor, University of Colorado
Spokesperson, American Dietetic Association

NUTRITIONAL PROFILE COMPARISON

Per serving	Nutrient Rich	Vegetarian	Old Style
calories	128	99	294
fat (g)	6	5	19
saturated fat (g)	2	2	9
carbohydrates (g)	6	7	11
fiber (g)	1	1	0
sodium (mg)	400	178	1108

Don't buy into any unbalanced program for eating and dieting, like the popular high protein/low carbohydrate diets. Instead, consider a balanced diet of food that will make you healthy, and strive to achieve this healthy mix each day. You can do this so easily with the help of a registered dietitian.

Since muscle tissue weighs more than fat mass, deceptive and detrimental weight loss is generally the result.

So, how much protein do you need each day to enjoy good health?

* Here's a handy 'formula': 0.8 grams of protein per kilogram of body weight = the number of grams of protein needed each day.
* When calculating your protein intake, be cautious when reading food labels. Be aware that the grams of protein listed on food labels is for one serving, so if you consume a package that serves two, you will need to double the amount of protein grams listed on the package. Ounce for ounce, all animal foods have the same amount of protein (7 grams per ounce). What differs is the fat content. For vegetarians, beans, grains, yogurt, milk, and peanut butter along with bread are all great sources of protein, but be aware that when you cut out dairy completely, you cut out important calcium sources. There are many products such as soy milk and cereals that have been fortified with calcium you might consider.

For more information on these and other important nutrition issues: call The American Dietetic Association 1-800-366-1655 or visit www.eatright.org

Crab Cakes
Oxford, Maryland

Losing weight is one tough thing to do. Keeping the weight off is tougher. Treena and I have had success by halving the portion sizes of the typical meal. One whole English muffin becomes one half with a teaspoon less of jam, a sandwich becomes open faced, four ounces dry weight of pasta becomes two. We found that this one decision saved us between 300 and 650 calories per day — between 100,000 and 250,000 calories per year!

At one time in our lives, Treena and I lived near Oxford, Maryland on Chesapeake Bay where crabbing is a way of life. Later (several homes later!), we found ourselves with a small beachfront on Camano Island on Puget Sound in the Pacific Northwest, where crabbing can be even more than a way of life! Of course, the crabs differ from the Chesapeake blues to the Dungeness reds, and so, for that matter, do the local renditions of the famous crab cakes. Mine have borrowed from the best and then been pressed into reason. Crab cakes seem innocent enough, but it's incredible that the old style version can pack up to 40 grams of fat and well over 500 calories . . . and they are usually appetizers! Mine do really well (taste and texture wise) at 5 grams of fat and half the calories. I'm totally delighted with the result. This is a must try, no matter where you live.

Appetizers

Ingredients:

1/4 cup finely chopped sweet onion
1/4 cup finely chopped celery
1/4 cup finely chopped red bell pepper
1/4 cup lightly packed chopped parsley
1/2 teaspoon dried thyme
16 unsalted top saltines, crushed
   (3/4 cup)
1/2 cup nonfat yogurt cheese
   (see 'The Basics')
1 teaspoon horseradish pinch saffron
1 tablespoon freshly squeezed lemon juice
2 tablespoons egg substitute
1 pound lump crabmeat
1 tablespoon paprika
1 bunch watercress, stemmed
2 cups mixed salad greens
1/4 cup peanut vinaigrette

Peanut Vinaigrette
1 clove garlic, bashed and chopped
2 tablespoons non-aromatic olive oil
1/2 cup rice wine vinegar
1/2 teaspoon dry mustard
1 teaspoon brown sugar
2 tablespoons peanut butter
1/8 teaspoon cayenne

Crab Cakes

1. Combine the onion, celery, pepper, parsley, thyme, cracker crumbs, yogurt, horseradish, saffron, lemon juice, and egg substitute. Stir the crab in gently.

2. Spray a flat baking sheet with olive oil spray. Sprinkle paprika over the whole pan. Pack the crab mixture tightly into a 1/3 cup measure and then tap it out onto the pan. Flatten each one to make 8, 3/4" thick patties. Turn and sprinkle the other sides with more paprika.

3. Heat a large skillet on medium high. Spray with olive oil pan spray and lay the patties in the hot pan. Sprinkle additional paprika lightly on the tops. Fry for 3 minutes on each side. Combine the watercress and salad greens and divide among 4 plates. Drizzle with peanut dressing and top with 2 crab cakes.

Serves 4

National Weight Registry

Professor James Hill and Dr Holly Thompson-Wyatt stopped by to report on the findings of the 'National Weight Registry' which collects data on people who have lost over 30 pounds — and kept it off for at least one year. Now, these people are 'real' losers! We all got a lot of hope from their simple success stories . . . hey, the current 15-20% success rate for those trying to lose weight is a whole lot better than the previously reported 5–10%. Now, how do you plan a recipe for them!

Why take action if you are overweight?

There are 300,000 preventable deaths a year in North America caused by overeating (that is 8 times the AIDS death rate).

What have we learned from these' real' losers?

There are over 3,000 successful people in the National Weight Registry database and the numbers are growing. In the past, the success rate of dropping this weight and keeping it off for one year was 5-10%, but this has grown to 15-20%. While there is no simple relationship between how people lost the weight and their ability to maintain it, there are some methods that worked better than others

What seems to work?

For those who have maintained their weight loss, there were three practices in common:
* Eating lowfat foods (24% of calories from fat).
* Watching total calories in addition to the low fat diet.
* Exercising (60-90 minutes a day).

By following this lifestyle you don't have to be so concerned about every little thing you eat and can still find pleasure in your food. By keeping track of your food intake and weighing yourself regularly, you can pick up problems earlier and you can develop a strategy to solve them. Make exercise a priority, and remember that it can be done throughout the day. Research has shown that as you lose weight, metabolism is regulated appropriately.

For more information on this topic: call 1-800-606-NWCR

James Hill, PhD
Professor and Director, Colorado Clinical Nutrition Research Unit

Holly Thompson-Wyatt, MD
Assistant Professor, Department of Medicine, University of Colorado

NUTRITIONAL PROFILE COMPARISON

Per serving	Nutrient Rich	Old Style
calories	264	561
fat (g)	5	40
saturated fat (g)	1	10
carbohydrates (g)	20	20
fiber (g)	3	2
sodium (mg)	555	933

There are a lot of ways to lose weight,

but the key to being successful is to make

a 'chronic' lifestyle change that you can

maintain for a lifetime.

Cannery Scallops Claudia
Vancouver, British Columbia

*H*ave you ever wondered why home-made traditional comfort foods are so comforting? Is it the feeling that someone actually created the meal from their own imagination with their own hands? Is it because we have a culinary cultural memory that recalls the flavor of these meals? Or could it be that we instinctively know this food is good for our health? Culinary mysteries yet to be solved!

I had a wonderful time with Fredrick Couton, the Executive Chef at Vancouver's famous "Cannery Restaurant" down past the gaslight district on the docks at Commission and Victoria Drive. I wanted Chef Couton, a French born culinarian with Asian experiences, to do his own thing for the camera, no restrictions except that the completed dish would be both delicious and would not wound. Both Treena and I loved the final outcome and so appreciated Fredrick, especially since he did all this on a very rare day off. We all agreed, by the way, that the dish should be named after his wife Claudia, because she too sacrificed her time with Frederick to make this possible. The dish is extraordinary and not at all as hard as it may look at first glance.

Appetizers

Ingredients:

Barley
1/2 teaspoon non-aromatic olive oil
1 heaped tablespoon coarsely chopped
   lemon grass
1 tablespoon chopped fresh ginger
1 1/2 cups water
1 tablespoon Thai fish sauce
1/2 cup pearl barley
1 cup corn kernels
2 tablespoons chopped fresh parsley

Seafood
1 1/2 teaspoons non-aromatic olive oil,
   divided
1 stalk lemon grass, trimmed and finely
   sliced (cut by sliding knife along the grain
   of the bulb to give you fine shavings)
1/4 cup finely chopped shallots
1/4 cup chopped fresh basil, divided
1 kafir lime leaf, fine sliced or 1 strip
   lime zest
1-pound (450 g) mussels,
   scrubbed and bearded
1 cup de-alcoholized chardonnay
1/8 teaspoon cayenne pepper
1/8 teaspoon toasted sesame oil
1/2 teaspoon Thai fish sauce
8 medium sea scallops
1/2-pound (225 g) medium shrimp, peeled
2 teaspoons arrowroot mixed with 1/4 cup
   de-alcoholized white wine (slurry)
2 teaspoons freshly squeezed lime juice

Cannery Scallops Claudia

1. Heat the oil in a saucepan on medium high. Add the lemon grass and ginger and cook 1 minute to release the flavors. Add the water and fish sauce and bring to a boil. Cover and set off the heat 4 minutes. Remove the lemon grass and ginger. Add the barley, bring back to a boil, reduce the heat, cover and simmer 20 minutes. Add the corn and cook 5 more minutes. Set aside and keep warm until ready to serve.

2. Heat 1/2 teaspoon of the oil in a large skillet or chef's pan on medium high. Add the lemon grass, shallots, 2 tablespoons of the basil, and the lime leaf or zest. Sauté 2 minutes to break out the flavors. Drop in the mussels and pour in the wine. Cover and cook 2 1/2 minutes or until the mussels open. Remember seafood is cooked in order to develop the flavor and not to make it tender because seafood is tender to begin with. Strain, reserving the liquid and place the mussels on a plate to cool. Remove the meats and set aside.

3. Add the cayenne, sesame oil and fish sauce. Return the liquid in the pan and simmer 10 minutes. Strain the liquid and reserve.

4. Reheat the pan. Add another 1/2 teaspoon of the oil. Drop the scallops into the pan to brown, about 2 minutes per side. Remove to a hot plate and cover to finish cooking. Heat the remaining oil. Add the shrimp and cook until the first one turns pink, adding a little of the reserved liquid if the pan is too dry. Turn and cook 1 minute more. Pour in the remaining reserved liquid. Stir in the slurry and heat to thicken. Add the rest of the basil, reserved mussel meats, and scallops. Add the lime juice to brighten the flavors.

5. Divide the barley and corn mixture among 4 hot plates. Arrange the seafood attractively on top and spoon just a little of the sauce over the shellfish. Scatter more chopped basil or parsley over the top. Lightly steamed sugar snap peas are a lovely addition to this dish.

Serves 4

Multicultural Food Guide Pyramids

K. Dun Gifford appeared on the show to enlighten us about Oldways Preservation and Exchange Trust, an organization that promotes the value of 'old ways' of cooking food and the cultural traditions that go with them. We instinctively know that 'old ways' meals are good for us — that's why we take such comfort in traditional comfort foods. But all too often we eat against our instincts and forget the old ways — to our peril.

What is the aim of Oldways Preservation and Exchange Trust?

We wanted to offer a highly palatable, healthful framework for dietary change and establish for the first time a scientific basis for the preservation and revitalization of traditional diets. We can gain so much by valuing the 'old ways' of cooking food and the traditions that go with them. Through international education programs we demonstrate the contemporary significance of humanity's agricultural, culinary, and dietary legacies and show how the lessons of the past can be applied to address present-day needs. We have found that you must synergize with the scientific, culinary, and environmental communities to create clear-cut information to educate people.

What else has Oldways discovered?

* People want 'real food', whole and fresh, as the tremendous growth in the number and size of Farmers Markets shows.
* People who eat a traditional Mediterranean diet, featuring pasta, rice, crusty breads, and Greek salads, and who exercise regularly have lower rates of heart disease and cancer.
* Whole grains, fruits and vegetables, and fish are the base of a healthy diet with smaller amounts of sugars and red meat. Olives and olive oil are healthful in small amounts.
* The lowfat mania has caused significant health problems. While saturated fat should be eliminated, other fats are healthy in moderate amounts. Oldways stands by the research which shows around 25-35% of calories from fat is appropriate.
* Sensible eating is a balance of fats, carbohydrates, and protein.

K. Dun Gifford, JD
President and Director, Oldways Preservation and Exchange Trust

NUTRITIONAL PROFILE COMPARISON

Per serving	Nutrient Rich	Old Style
calories	399	525
fat (g)	7	28
saturated fat (g)	1	11
carbohydrates (g)	54	33
fiber (g)	4	2
sodium (mg)	848	810

We should all work together to encourage the preservation and popularization of traditional foods, foodways, and diets that are healthy, environmentally sustainable, and culturally significant. By maintaining this effort, all people can eat healthfully with real food that is nutritious, delicious, satisfying, and fun.

* We realize that one size doesn't fit all with diets and a wide variety of foods in the diet will prove to be of great benefit to achieving optimal health over time.

What are 'Food Guide Pyramids' for various cuisines that Oldways has created?

* Vegetarian
* African American
* Latin American
* Mediterranean
* Asian

For more information on this topic: www.oldwayspt.org or call 617-621-3000.

Tortilla Soup
San Antonio, Texas

*I*t's a brave new world, and a major innovation in the culinary world is what we now call 'functional foods'. Basically, a functional food is a commonly used food that is 'boosted' by the manufacturer to give you more nutrition per ounce, especially in areas where you may be lacking certain nutrients. But for generations in many different culinary traditions, a common functional food has been 'chicken soup' (and not just for the soul!).

For more years than I care to announce, I've been making my own 'scratch' chicken stock by a classical French method taught to me in my dad's hotel when I was about 12 years old. Recently, reading Rick Bayless' account on the subject in his great book, aptly called the Mexican Kitchen, I was struck by his notes on the difference in the way it is made south of the border. Here's the basic broth recipe from the modern master of the Mexican menu (how's that for alliteration?), Rick Bayless.

Soups

Ingredients:

Mexican Chicken Broth

1 teaspoon non-aromatic olive oil
1 medium sweet onion, thinly sliced
3 cloves garlic, peeled and halved
1 whole chicken, quartered
4 1/2 quarts water
Bouquet Garni (see "The Basics')

Ingredients:

Tortilla Soup

4 corn tortillas, cut in 1/8" (1/4 cm) strips
2 cloves unpeeled garlic
3 dried pasilla chiles, stemmed, and seeded
2 Roma tomatoes, cored, halved, and seeded
1 teaspoon non-aromatic olive oil
1 sweet onion, thinly sliced
6 cups Mexican Chicken Broth, divided
1/2 teaspoon salt
4 cups loosely packed, thinly sliced Swiss chard leaves, stems removed reserved breast meat from broth, sliced across the grain
1 lime, cut in wedges

Mexican Chicken Broth

(adapted from Rick Bayless' *Mexican Kitchen*)

1. Heat the oil in a large stockpot on medium high. Drop in the onion to sauté 2 or 3 minutes. Add the garlic and cook 1 minute more.

2. Place bouquet garni in a tea ball and drop on top of the onions. Lay the chicken pieces on top and pour on the water.

3. Bring to a boil, skimming off the foam as it rises to the top. Reduce the heat and simmer 20 minutes. Take out the breast pieces, remove the meat from the bones and refrigerate. Return the breast bones and skin to the pot, and continue simmering 1 hour and 40 minutes more.

4. Strain the broth, discarding the debris. Remove the fat with a fat strainer or chill and skim. The broth can be frozen.

Makes a generous 2 quarts.

Serves 4

Tortilla Soup

We went to San Antonio to find the famed Caldo or Tortilla Soup. This is about as basic and caring and comforting as you can get. It finds its unique place somewhere between the Jewish Chicken Soup and the Thai Tom Yum Gai for a truly invigorating, appetite enhancing, spicy delicacy. The addition of the chard was, by the way, another 'trick from Rick'(Bayless no less!).

1. Preheat the oven to 425°F (220°C). Scatter the tortilla strips on a greased baking sheet. Spray lightly with olive oil pan spray. Set the un-peeled garlic cloves on the sheet, too. Bake 10 to 15 minutes or until the tortillas are crisp and the garlic soft. Set aside.

2. Heat a heavy bottomed skillet on medium high. Toast the chiles lightly, just 30 seconds or until little curls of smoke rise from the pan. Place 1 of the chiles in a bowl of hot water to rehydrate 30 minutes. Chop the other two finely for garnish. Reheat the pan and roast the tomato halves skin side down until dark and blistered. Turn to darken the other side. Set aside.

3. Heat the oil in a large saucepan on medium high. Fry the onion until golden, 5 to 7 minutes. Drain the rehydrated chile and place in a blender jar. Add the peeled roasted garlic, roasted tomatoes, and 1 cup of the broth. Whiz until smooth. Press the puree through a strainer into the onions. Stir until dark and thick. Pour in the remaining broth and simmer, uncovered, 30 minutes. Stir in the chard and simmer until tender, 5 to 6 minutes. Just before you serve, add the chicken breast to heat through.

4. Arrange the tortilla strips, chopped chiles, and lime wedges on a plate. Divide the soup among 4 hot soup plates and serve. Pass the garnish.

Functional Foods

To underscore the information on functional foods Registered Dietitian and Professor Cyndi Thomson was bringing us, I made her this traditional Mexican chicken soup. Chicken soup may be more 'psycho-nutrient' than the typical scientifically constructed foods, but it gave us a comforting place to begin.

What are 'functional foods' and 'fortified foods'?

Foods we eat everyday, but which have been modified or enhanced in some way to make them more healthful. Fortified foods are usually government issued, and the government makes a decision that a food needs to be fortified, such as grains with B vitamins. Functional foods are the manufacturer's decision to enhance the food in order to market it for the health benefit.

How can 'functional foods' be of benefit to our health?

They are designed for those who are having difficulty getting all the nutrients that they need from the traditional foods that we eat — and that includes many of us!
* Cereals have traditionally been enhanced and fortified with non-essential nutrients not always available in other foods.
* Orange juice has calcium added because we may not get enough calcium throughout the day.
* Energy bars are designed to enhance sports performance with extra nutrients but not as a replacement for a meal.

Cyndi Thomson, PhD, RD
Researcher/Lecturer, Arizona Prevention Center, University of Arizona
Spokesperson, American Dietetic Association

NUTRITIONAL PROFILE COMPARISON

Per serving	Nutrient Rich	Old Style
calories	281	590
fat (g)	5	35
saturated fat (g)	1	13
carbohydrates (g)	24	24
fiber (g)	5	5
sodium (mg)	714	1093

At the supermarket look at the contents of your basket for the colors of the rainbow which will often indicate wise choices and lots of nutrient-dense foods.

* Eggs have been supplemented with Omega-3 Fatty Acids.

How do you determine if you need to eat 'functional foods'?

A Registered Dietitian or Physician can be of great help to determine an individual's specific nutrient needs.
* Individual dietary guidelines can be established. Age differences, gender differences, and stress differences all play a role in determining individual needs.
* Whole foods and the nutrients that we receive from these foods cannot be replicated by pills, so we should focus our sights on getting optimal nutrition through the foods we eat.
* Medication along with certain food/nutrient interactions can affect individuals differently — another important reason to work with a qualified health professional as you work to improve your diet.

For further information on this topic contact: www.eatright.org

$\mathscr{S}$enate Bean Soup
Washington, DC

The 'table' adds to the pleasure and conversation we can experience when we are dining . . . without the table, we are forced to forgo some of life's greatest pleasures. Strive to make your 'gathering place' one of joy, celebration, and conversation for the enjoyment of food, enhancement of relationships, and appreciation of the pleasures of life.

The Capitol Hill dining rooms sustain US senators in their constant search for bi-partisan agreement — and for being voted back into office. Not always an easy balancing act! Making life a little more tolerable when the weather turns really cold is the now famous Navy Bean Soup introduced at Massachusetts Senator Henry Cabot Lodge's insistence. This is very hearty and healthy — and, I guess, bi-partisan! You can use several different types of beans for an attractive mottled appearance.

Ingredients:

1 pound smoky ham hock
8 cups water
1 bay leaf
3 whole cloves
1 pound navy beans, rinsed, picked over and
  soaked overnight (or 6 cups canned navy
  beans, rinsed and drained)
1/2 teaspoon non-aromatic olive oil
1 large sweet onion, chopped
4 cloves garlic, bashed and chopped
2 carrots, peeled and cut in 1/4" dice
  (1 1/2 cups)
2 ribs celery, cut in 1/4" dice (1 cup)
1 medium russet potato,
  peeled and chopped (1 1/2 cups)
1/2 teaspoon ground cumin
1/4 teaspoon dried summer savory
2 tablespoons chopped parsley
1/2 teaspoon salt (optional)
1/4 teaspoon pepper

Vegetarian Option Ingredients:

For the ham, water, bay leaf, and whole
cloves, substitute:
8 cups canned or homemade low sodium
  vegetable broth (see 'The Basics')
3 teaspoons, rinsed, seeded and chopped
  canned chipotle chile (pronounced
  'phi-oat-lay') or chipotle sauce to taste
  (available in dried form and in cans with
  adobo sauce)

Senate Bean Soup

1. Cover the ham hock with 8 cups water in a large kettle. Toss in the bay and cloves and bring to a boil over high heat. Reduce the heat and simmer 1 1/2 hours or until the meat is tender. (You can do this step in a pressure cooker with the same ingredients and cooked for 30 minutes.) Strain the resulting stock into a fat strainer to remove the fat. Pour the de-fatted liquid back into the soup kettle, adding water to make 8 cups. Add the beans, bring to a boil, reduce the heat and simmer another 1 1/2 hours or until the beans are tender but not mushy. (This, too, can be accomplished in a pressure cooker. Check the manufacturers instructions for time.) Cut the meat from the ham hock to put into the soup later and discard the fat, skin and bone.

2. Heat the oil in a chef's pan or skillet on medium high. Saute the onion for 2 minutes and then add the garlic, carrots, celery and potato. Cook for 3 more minutes before adding to the cooked beans. Stir in the cumin and savory and simmer 20 minutes or until the vegetables are tender.

3. Pour about 1/3 of the bean mixture into a blender and whiz until smooth. Return it to the rest of the beans and stir in the reserved meat, parsley, salt and pepper. Serve with more chopped parsley.

Serves 6

Vegetarian Option: Senate Bean Soup

1. Heat the oil in a soup kettle on medium high. Saute the onion for 2 minutes and then add the garlic, carrots, celery, and potato. Cook for 3 more minutes before adding to the cooked beans. Pour in the vegetable stock and beans. Stir in the cumin and savory and simmer 20 minutes or until the vegetables are tender.

2 Pour about 1/3 of the bean mixture into a blender and whiz until smooth. Return it to the rest of the beans and stir in the parsley, pepper, and chipotle. Taste before adding salt as the canned beans and vegetable stock may be quite salty. Serve with more chopped parsley.

Culinary History

In pursuit of greater knowledge of culinary history, we invited Professor Albert Sonnenfeld to the Gathering Place. The co-author of Food: A Culinary History, Albert emphasized the value of table rituals in creating our sense of family and personal well-being. So, we gathered 'round' the table on our set and discussed the history of dining while we tasted Senate Bean Soup. All bipartisan and egalitarian!

Has the 'table' always been at the center of our dining experience?

Historically, we started without the dining table. The classical Greeks, for example, had carts for food and they would lie around on couches while dining. Aristocrats would sit at a higher elevation which gave us the notion that 'noble' foods are farthest from the ground. The table itself came from Christian culture where the altar plays a central role in the ritual of communion. The round table was designed as a symbol of egalitarianism, to show that everyone gathered round is an equal. Today, the most common formal dining table is arranged with a host at the head of the table, most noted guest to the left or right.

Albert Sonnenfeld, PhD
Chevalier Professor, French and Comparative
Literatures, University of Southern California,
Co-Author, *Food: A Culinary History*

What is the role of the table in our culture today?

Since its inception, the table has been used as a place where people could gather to share food. The table is the epicenter of our family relationships and our communion with friends. But this role of the table has changed over the past few decades. When you think about the fast food-drive through, the focus is on speed with lines to order the food, with uncomfortable seating so that you do not stay long. You bus your own table, and you are out the door in 10 minutes. Schools serve meals buffet-style, which leaves no room for conversation and very few pauses in the process. Increasingly we hear that families are not verbal at the table; children learn that conversation is no longer a role of family meals. Communication among family members declines, and the television takes over for many at mealtime.

NUTRITIONAL PROFILE COMPARISON

Per serving	Nutrient Rich	Vegetarian	Old Style
calories	292	275	448
fat (g)	4	2	8
saturated fat (g)	1	0.274	3
carbohydrates (g)	50	52	69
fiber (g)	2	2	3
sodium (mg)	205	175	759

The lure of the table is infinite . . .
Table rituals — manners, cutlery, place
settings, even the shape of the table —
have evolved throughout the history of
civilization, from classical Greek to
contemporary fast food culture.

What other culinary trends do you see developing?

Increasingly, we have a wealth of foods and flavors to experience derived from the growing ethnic diversity of our society, but rather than creating culinary diversity, such 'globalization' brings us closer and closer to the standardization of everything, including food. Local and regional flavors can be lost with the onslaught of readily-available fast, easy, economical, and familiar foods.

What can we do to preserve regional dietary diversity and this whole world of flavors?

Food books and cookbooks are the best selling titles in the publication world, and with shows like *Graham Kerr's Gathering Place* we will continue to be challenged to explore creatively the food we prepare and enjoy.

Mulligatawny Soup

Victoria, British Columbia

*I*t's called 'middle age spread' . . . it may begin with 'love handles' and advance to 'jelly belly' . . . but in one way or another it seems to happen to most of us. While we may want to lose our apple shaped middle for appearance's sake — and for our health's sake — there is no one diet or exercise that can remove this spot. Spot reduction may not work, but eating less and exercising more will result in overall weight loss, which is good for the heart and your health.

This soup is substantial and highly aromatic, a classic example of early attempts at 'fusion' cooking. When British military officers and diplomats returned from service in India, they brought along this great, somewhat spicy, coconut-flavored soup. It took root and became distinctly British and 'unusually' healthy!

Ingredients:

4 cups low sodium chicken stock
4 chicken thighs (1/4 pound or 227 g each)
1 teaspoon non-aromatic olive oil
1 medium onion, thinly sliced
2 cloves garlic, bashed and chopped
4 teaspoons curry powder
1 1/2 cups chopped parsnips (1 large)
1/2 cup dried red or brown lentils
1 bay leaf
1 pound (454 grams) broccoli, florets
 removed, stems peeled and chopped
1/4 teaspoon salt
1 cup cooked long grain white rice
3/4 cup Graham's coconut cream

Coconut Cream
3/4 cup 2% milk
1/2 teaspoon sugar
2 tablespoons unsweetened
 desiccated coconut
1 tablespoon cornstarch mixed with 2
 tablespoons 2% milk (slurry)
1/2 teaspoon natural coconut flavoring

Mulligatawny Soup

1. Place the thighs in a high-sided skillet and pour the stock over them. Cover, bring to a boil, reduce the heat, and simmer 35 minutes. Remove the thighs to a plate and pour the stock into a fat strainer. Set aside to use in step 2.

2. Heat the oil in the same skillet on medium high. Sauté the onion for 1 minute, add the garlic and curry and cook 2 more minutes. Stir in the parsnips, lentils, and bay leaf. De-fat the stock and add enough water to make 4 cups. Pour into the pan, cover, bring to a boil, reduce the heat and simmer 15 minutes or until the parsnips are soft. Add the broccoli florets and stems and simmer 5 more minutes.

3. Remove the skin and bones from the thighs and add the meat to the soup. Stir in the rice and 1/2 cup of the coconut cream. Heat to serving temperature and ladle into bowls. Top each with a dollop of the remaining coconut cream.

Cooking the Coconut Cream:

Combine the milk, sugar and coconut in a small saucepan and simmer 10 minutes. Strain and discard the coconut. Stir the slurry and coconut flavoring into the warm milk. Heat on medium, stirring until thickened. Set aside to cool.

Serves 6

Spot Reduction

The author of The Fidget Factor, Professor Victor L. Katch, visited our show to talk about fat and to explore the claim that spot reduction works to lose weight across the middle or the hips. Not only did he answer our question 'categorically', he gave us a host of hints for exercising to burn fat and maintain weight loss. Now I can get to work on that extra five pounds or so I've accumulated around the middle, my reserve in case of a possible famine! Start fidgeting.

Victor L. Katch, PhD
Professor of Kinesiology, University of Michigan
Author, The Fidget Factor and Exercise Physiology: Energy, Nutrition and Human Performance

What is fat?

* Fat cells looks like a water droplet and contain essential fatty acids required for good health. Most physically mature adult fat cells are fixed at age 18-21 years. Fat cells can increase in size (hypertrophy), and they shrink when we lose weight.

* Most of our fat is located in the abdominal region as a result of genetics, and fat accrues here as we age. For women, fat is concentrated in the lower abdomen and hips, creating a characteristic 'pear' shape, while for men, this extra fat gives an 'apple' shape to the upper abdomen.

Do spot reduction diets and exercises work to reduce this fat ?

Spot Reduction does not work! Research shows there is no selective use of calories for various parts of the body. Instead calories are utilized by the body as a whole. Also, no additional weight is lost from certain areas of the body just because of more muscle tone. Even 5,000 sit-ups won't result in more weight loss in the stomach versus the arm.

So, what is the most effective way to reduce excess fat?

The most effective way to lose weight is a combination of decreasing calories consumed and increasing calories expended — in other words, more exercise and less food. Exercise not only provides immediate calorie expenditure but also speeds up metabolism so that you burn more calories even at rest. As we lose weight, fat comes off the whole body proportionally, beginning from the largest fat-containing area on the body. So, whether you walk, run, swim or fidget, the greatest amount of fat will be lost in the area where you have the greatest fat stores.

NUTRITIONAL PROFILE COMPARISON

Per serving	Nutrient Rich	Old Style
calories	290	281
fat (g)	7	18
saturated fat (g)	2	4
carbohydrates (g)	32	7
fiber (g)	8	1
sodium (mg)	204	725

Spot reduction does not work! Instead, move the whole body as often as possible. Find enjoyable ways to move the large muscles on your body — and remember that if weight loss is your goal, whole body exercises are best for increasing calorie expenditure, too.

What exercise plan do you recommend to create the 'flat stomach' we see promoted in all kinds of fitness and fashion advertisements these days?

1. Move a little more and eat a little less.

2. Do sit-ups to increase muscle, because the more muscle we have the more fat we burn.

What exercise do you recommend for overall optimal health?

1. Exercise daily, enough to expend 300 calories. For example, walk about 3 miles a day, or undertake another kind of exercise for approximately 30-45 minutes a day.

2. Fidget often — for example, walk in place while standing in line. People who fidget can lose 8-12 pounds a year.

For more information on this topic: contact the division of Kinesiology at the University of Michigan at www.umich.edu

Creamy & Manhattan Clam Chowder

Boston, Massachusetts & New York, New York

Stressed out! Research shows us that there is a direct relationship between stress and our body's internal biochemical changes. Managing stress can result in better health — enhanced physical and behavioral outcomes. But remember, we cannot eliminate stress totally; some stress is a good thing and can challenge us to make positive, healthy choices!

Now frankly, being a West coaster, I'm not associated 'strongly' with the factions that have set up very real boundaries between the Manhattan and the Boston (or New England clam chowders). I'm inclined, on the basis of T.A.C.T.(taste, aroma, color and texture) to prefer the Manhattan, with all its teaming colors and textures, but I can easily see how the puritan white, glossy, creamy, buttery Northern clam chowder has its devotees and perhaps its pure validity, coming as it does from the French La Chaudiere, a Northern French dish that would certainly have been based upon local butter and cream. In this case I'll simply opt for both and let you fight it out (if you feel you must!) Please note, however, my small intervention at suggesting smoked salmon as a creative alternative to the salt pork or bacon. I prefer a lightly smoked sockeye in both dishes.

Soups

Ingredients:

Creamy Clam Chowder

4 1/2-pounds (2 kg) small live clams
2 cups water
1/2 teaspoon non-aromatic olive oil
4-ounces (113 gm) Canadian bacon, cut in 1/2" dice
1 large sweet onion, chopped (2 cups)
1 1/2-pounds (675 gm) medium red potatoes,
   peeled and cut in 3/4" (2 cm) dice (4 cups)
1 bay leaf
1/2 teaspoon dried thyme
1/4 teaspoon freshly ground black pepper
3 cups 1% milk
1/3 cup cornstarch mixed with
   2/3 cup water (slurry)
1 can, 12-fluid ounce (354 ml), nonfat
   evaporated milk

Ingredients:

Manhattan Clam Chowder

1 teaspoon non-aromatic olive oil
2-ounces Canadian bacon, cut in 1/4" (.75 cm) dice
1 large sweet onion, chopped (2 cups)
4 carrots, peeled and chopped (1 1/2 cups)
2 ribs celery, chopped (3/4 cup)
3 cups Yellow Finn or Yukon Gold potatoes,
   peeled and cut in 3/4" (2 cm) dice
2 cans, 10-ounce (283 gm), small whole clams,
   drained, juice reserved
1 8-fluid ounce (236 ml) bottle clam juice
1/4 teaspoon freshly ground black pepper
1/2 teaspoon dried thyme
1 bay leaf
2-pounds (900 mg) Roma tomatoes, peeled,
   seeded and cut in 3/4" (2 cm) dice
2 tablespoons chopped parsley

Creamy Clam Chowder

1. Rinse the clams, scrub if need be. Bring the water to a boil in a large skillet. Add the clams, cover and bring back to the boil. Cook 5 minutes or until the clams open. Discard the unopened ones. When they have cooled, drain, saving the liquid, and pick out the meats. Strain the liquid through cheesecloth if you see any sand. You should have 2 cups of clams and 3 cups juice. Add water to make the 3 cups if you are short.

2. Heat the oil in a Dutch oven on medium high. Sauté the bacon until brown, 1 to 2 minutes. Add the onions and cook 3 minutes or until they start turning translucent. Stir in the potatoes, bay leaf, thyme, and pepper. Pour in the reserved clam juice and milk and bring to a boil. Reduce the heat and simmer, uncovered, 10 minutes or until the potatoes are tender.

3. Stir in the slurry and boil 30 seconds to thicken. Add the evaporated milk and reserved clams, and heat. It is traditional to serve light water crackers on the side but with nearly 50 grams of carbohydrates in the chowder, there seems little reason other than texture. Serve in hot soup bowls.

Serves 6

Manhattan Clam Chowder

1. Heat the oil in a Dutch oven on medium high. Drop in the bacon to fry 1 minute, then the onions to cook 2 or 3 minutes more. Add the carrots, celery and potatoes, stir and sauté 3 minutes. Pour in the reserved clam nectar and clam juice. Season with the pepper, thyme, and bay leaf. Bring to a boil then simmer 10 minutes or until the potatoes and carrots are tender.

2. Stir in the tomatoes and parsley and bring to a boil again. Cook 2 to 3 minutes to let the tomatoes cook down a little. Add the clams and serve. The chowder will be thick and stew like.

Serves 6

Stress, Blood Sugar & Health

After watching me prepare two recipes for one show, psychologist Jeff Janata informed me that extraordinary stress does adversely affect our emotional and physical well-being! Then he 'stressed' the value of good nutrition and exercise for controlling stress. That's enough stress for me for one day.

How does stress affect our health?

Stress can affect our health significantly:

* Stress affects physical mechanisms including internal/hormonal changes as well as behavioral mechanisms.

* Research on medical students (a highly stressed population) shows us that there was a clear deterioration of auto-immune function during exam time, which was a physical manifestation of stress.

* Stress can influence blood glucose regulation.

* 'Stressed' people are much more susceptible to illness, colds, and flu.

* Stress can make us more irritable so that we don't act in an even-tempered way.

* Under stress, we may not think as well.

* In some cases, stress may impair our overall daily ability to function.

How do we handle stress?

We need to begin to care for ourselves knowing that stress has such a powerful impact on our lives and our health:

* Learn to care for yourself in a positive and pro-healthy way.

* Exercise, proper nutrition and an overall understanding of your health is a great start.

* Stress management counseling can give you tools to make optimal choices for your health.

* Find exercise that you enjoy and will allow you to continue, consistently — this is exercise that can positively affect your stress level.

For further information on this topic contact: http://www.apa.org/psychnet/

Jeff Janata, PhD
Psychologist, University Hospitals of Cleveland

NUTRITIONAL PROFILE COMPARISON CREAMY		
Per serving	Nutrient Rich	Old Style
calories	323	800
fat (g)	3	39
saturated fat (g)	1	20
carbohydrates (g)	49	66
fiber (g)	3	5
sodium (mg)	1239	2331

NUTRITIONAL PROFILE COMPARISON MANHATTAN		
Per serving	Nutrient Rich	Old Style
calories	192	440
fat (g)	3	21
saturated fat (g)	1	7
carbohydrates (g)	31	37
fiber (g)	5	6
sodium (mg)	706	1996

runswick Stew

New Brunswick, Canada

*F*at is vital to our health, but it's one of those nutritional conundrums — we can't live without it, but if we eat too much of it, fat can contribute to coronary disease, obesity, diabetes, even cancer. We must learn to live with 'fat' — all within reason.

Living on the Canadian/American border as I do in the Pacific Northwest, I really enjoy the best of both worlds! It's because of these benefits that I'm loath to spark a dispute, especially over this famous chicken stew! Is it Brunswick County, North Carolina or Brunswick County, Virginia where it used to be made with squirrels? There's even a mild rumor that it may have begun its days up in New Brunswick, Canada and simply drifted south with the trappers. Whatever the truth, nobody seems to know. The fact is, it's delicious and with all its twists and turns, has become a genuine North American comfort food.

Main Dishes

Ingredients:

1 frying chicken (3 1/2-pound or 1.5 kg) or 2
  boneless skinless breasts and 2 hindquarters
1 teaspoon non-aromatic olive oil, divided
1 large sweet onion cut in 1" (2 1/2 cm) dice
  (generous 2 cups)
3 ribs celery cut in 1/4" (3/4 cm) slices
  (1 1/2 cups)
3-ounces Canadian bacon, cut the same size
  as the celery
1 red bell pepper cut the same
2 cups canned, crushed tomatoes
1 cup canned or homemade low sodium
  chicken stock (see 'The Basics')
1 tablespoon Worcestershire sauce
1/4 teaspoon cayenne pepper
1 cup frozen baby lima beans
1 cup frozen corn kernels
1 tablespoon arrowroot mixed with
  2 tablespoons stock or water (slurry)
1/4 cup chopped fresh parsley
1/4 cup chopped fresh basil

Brunswick Stew

1. If you are using a whole chicken, cut off the legs with the thighs and the breasts. Use the carcass and wings for stock. Remove the skin from all the pieces. Separate the legs from the thighs and bone the thigh, leaving the bone in the leg. Remove the skin and bone from the breast pieces. Bones, fat and skin will all help to make a flavorful stock. Cut the meat into 1 1/2" (4 cm) chunks.

2. Heat 1/2 teaspoon of the oil in a 10 1/2" chef's pan on medium high. Sauté the onion 3 minutes or until starting to turn translucent. Add the celery, Canadian bacon, and red bell pepper and cook 3 more minutes. Remove to a plate and without washing the pan, add the remaining 1/2 teaspoon oil and heat. When the pan is nice and hot, toss in the thigh meat and legs to brown 2 minutes. Add the breast meat and brown 1 to 2 minutes more.

3. Pour in the tomatoes, stock, and Worcestershire sauce. Add the cooked vegetables and cayenne. Bring to a boil, reduce the heat, cover and simmer 35 minutes or until the chicken is tender. Add the lima beans and corn and cook 12 minutes more or until the beans are tender. Stir in the slurry and heat to thicken. Add the parsley and basil and you are ready to serve.

Serves 6

Fat Facts

Fats that Heal, Fats that Kill *is the title of a popular book by author Udo Erasmus. Which fats are good? Which are bad? These are the questions we posed to Registered Dietitian Connie Diekman when she appeared on The Gathering Place.*

Connie Diekman, MEd, FADA, RD
Spokesperson, American Dietetic Association

What is the nutritional role of fat in our diet?

Fat as an essential component of our diet, and thus we need to determine the amount and type of fat we need for optimal health. Essential fatty acids are necessary to make hormones. Many vitamins are only fat soluble (vitamin A,D,E, K), and we need vitamin D, for example, to get calcium into the bones. Fat is one of a number of ingredients that add flavor to our foods, making it more appetizing.

What fats are the best choices?

1. Animal fats in meats and cheeses, for example, are saturated and can often cause cholesterol levels to rise. Limit your consumption of these fats.

2. Plant fats in nuts and olive oil, for example, are predominantly unsaturated and can cause cholesterol levels to go down. Choose a moderate amount of these fats for your diet.

Many fats are obvious in foods like butter, margarine, salad dressings, and olive oil, while others are 'hidden' in foods like cookies, crackers, chicken, cheese, and avocado. Limit butter and margarine, which are often saturated fats, choosing instead to use olive oil, a monounsaturated fat.

How much fat do we need on a daily basis?

General goals for daily fat intake to create optimal health differ for men and women:

Female	Male
1500 calories	2000 calories
50 grams fat (30%)	65 grams fat (30%)
41 grams fat (25%)	55 grams fat (25%)

These numbers provide a typical calorie value for women and men and a range of fat grams

NUTRITIONAL PROFILE COMPARISON

Per serving	Nutrient Rich	Old Style
calories	260	754
fat (g)	6	32
saturated fat (g)	2	15
carbohydrates (g)	21	57
fiber (g)	3	10
sodium (mg)	362	809

that correlate with the calorie intake. For cholesterol reduction or weight loss, you may lower fat grams even more. Check with your physician to see what is right for you.

How do we control fat in our diet?

* Look at the food guide pyramid and build up from the bottom (keep the smaller percent of calories from the top-fats).
* Look at your plate and divide it into 3/4-fruits, whole grains, vegetables and 1/4 -fat containing foods.
* See a Registered Dietitian to find the grams of fat that are right for you.

For more information: contact www.eatright.org or call 1-800-366-1655 to find a registered dietitian in your area.

$\mathcal{L}$amb Greystone
Napa, California

$\mathcal{I}$t is perfectly possible to eat a fabulous diet from what is available in the supermarkets. The food supply is abundant with healthy choices at reasonable prices and if consumed in a balanced way, should clearly result in better nutrition and reduced disease risk. Walk more, eat less — and most of all — enjoy food for the great pleasure that it can give to all who partake.

Treena and I visited Greystone (the west coast center of the Culinary Institute of America, located in the Napa Valley) just before Thanksgiving when 'all on the campus was quiet'. In fact, almost nothing stirred except for Chef Director Mark Erickson, a long time 'star' of CIA's Culinary Arts. Mark prepared this dish for the camera while everyone else got ready for the holiday. We had a wonderful time eating the superb dish in the midst of one of the most breathtaking kitchens on earth . . . in almost monastic silence. Do please try this one — it's delicious and it's a perfect example of adaptation of Mediterranean cuisine to fit a very similar Californian climate and agriculture.

Ingredients:

Polenta

2 cups canned or homemade low
  sodium chicken stock (see 'The Basics')
2 cups 1% milk
1 cup cornmeal or polenta
1/4 cup grated parmesan cheese
1/4 teaspoon salt

Filling

2 teaspoons non-aromatic olive oil, divided
8-ounces (227 g) lean ground lamb
1 onion cut in 1/4" (.75 cm) dice, (1 1/2 cups)
1 red bell pepper, cut in 1/2" (11/2 cm) dice (1 cup)
1 yellow bell pepper, cut in 1/2" (1.5 cm) dice
  (1 cup)
3 large cloves garlic, bashed and chopped
2 tablespoons tomato paste
1 small eggplant cut in 1/2" (1.5 cm) dice
  (3 cups)
1 medium zucchini, cut in quarters lengthwise
  then across in 1/2" (1.5 cm) chunks (1 cup)
1 yellow summer squash, cut in 1/2" (1.5 cm)
  chunks (1 cup)
1/4 cup + 1 teaspoon balsamic vinegar
1/2 cup chopped fresh basil
3 tablespoons chopped fresh oregano
1/4 teaspoon salt
1/4 teaspoon pepper
6 Roma tomatoes, cored, seeded and cut in 1/2"
  (1.5 cm) dice
2 tablespoons grated parmesan cheese
1 teaspoon arrowroot mixed with
  2 teaspoons water (slurry)

Lamb Greystone

1. Combine the chicken stock and milk in a 4 quart (1 liter) saucepan. Bring to a boil. Rain the cornmeal into the hot liquid, whisking constantly. Cook on low heat, stirring often, 30 minutes. Stir in parmesan cheese and salt and set aside.

2. Heat 1 teaspoon of the oil in a chef's pan or large skillet on medium high. Drop the ground lamb into the hot pan to brown, then tip out onto a plate. Heat the remaining oil and sauté the onion 2 minutes or until it begins to wilt. Add the peppers and garlic and cook 3 minutes more. Stir in the tomato paste and cook, stirring, until it darkens. Add the eggplant and stir to coat with the tomato paste. Toss in the eggplant, squash, reserved meat, 1/4 cup balsamic vinegar, basil, oregano, salt and pepper. Cover and simmer 15 to 20 minutes or until the vegetables are tender. Stir in the tomatoes and heat through. Preheat the oven to 350°F (180°C).

3. Grease a baking sheet with 1 flat side. Lay 6" flan rings on the pan and spray. Divide the polenta among the rings and press flat with the back of an oiled dessert spoon. Squeeze the liquid out of the filling and reserve it in the pan as you pack the vegetables gently into a 1 cup measure and turn out onto each tart. Scatter the parmesan over the filling and bake 15 to 20 minutes or until heated through.

4. Stir the slurry into the reserved liquid with the remaining balsamic vinegar to make a finishing sauce and heat to thicken. Slide the tarts to dinner plates and drizzle the sauce over each.

Serves 6

Vegetarian Option: Lamb Greystone

To make a vegetarian version of this dish, replace the chicken stock with vegetable stock in the polenta. Leave out the lamb in step 2 and replace it with 8-ounces (227 g) finely chopped mushrooms. Add them to the sautéed onions with the garlic and peppers and proceed with the rest of the recipe.

How Simple Is A Healthy Diet?

Here she is, another of my genuine, knock down, drag out food heroes (or rather, hero-ines)! Marion Nestle is a straight talker, who has cleared the way for millions of us 'lay' people to get a simple grasp on a healthy diet. One of her own all-time favorite cuisine styles is loosely described as 'Mediterranean', and while several cultures occupy its 'waterfront', most of them favor a variety of vegetables and grains, smaller amounts of meat, good seafood, olive oil, and truly heady, passionate, aromatic seasoning. Marion addressed some of the problems with our current diet.

What changes do we need to make in our diet to improve our health?

We need to make two changes in the typical adult diet:

* Balance calories through more activity and eating less food overall.

* Focus on incorporating more fruits and vegetables into a person's daily intake, so one can begin to move toward a more balanced and healthy diet.

Marion Nestle, PhD, MPH
Chair, Department of Nutrition, New York University

How can we create and maintain this focus?

We do need to make lifestyle changes to create lasting habits:

* We must think broadly. A diet that has a majority of calories from fruits, vegetables, and grains, a moderate use of milk, meat, and dairy products, and minimal use of fat, salt, and sugar is clearly associated with lower rates of disease.

* We are not suggesting eating specialty foods, but everyday foods you can easily pick up at the supermarket. Eat foods that you enjoy, but consider going outside your normal boundaries and try new foods.

* Don't overeat. We live in the era of super-stores, mega-deals, and huge food portions. We rarely need more than half the portion that is served. It really is simple, the bigger the portion, the more calories you will end up consuming! To keep your calories in check, there are some simple ways to reduce portions and eat less:

1. Cut a portion in half.

2. Don't buy the largest item.

3. Share your meal with someone else.

NUTRITIONAL PROFILE COMPARISON

Per serving	Nutrient Rich	Vegetarian	Old Style
calories	317	251	376
fat (g)	9	5	18
saturated fat (g)	3	2	6
carbohydrates (g)	40	42	33
fiber (g)	6	6	4
sodium (mg)	374	345	395

Eating a healthy diet is simple . . . the basic advice hasn't changed for 50 years . . . eat a plant-based diet. Strive to emphasize fresh fruits and vegetables, grains and legumes as the focus of your diet. Keep dairy and meat portions moderate and limit added fats and sugars.

* Exercise. You can gain 60-80% of the benefits with walking one mile a day, so it doesn't have to be a marathon and it doesn't even have to be running!

Making lifelong changes in your diet and lifestyle goals require only a partial commitment. Don't feel as though you have to do it all at once. Don't set unrealistic goals for yourself.

What's the problem with the 'fat free' craze?

People feel that if a food is fat free, they can consume as much as they want, but just because it is fat free, does not mean there are fewer calories. The 'fat free' mania has resulted in greater consumption of foods and total calories, leading to weight gain. The key is that we're not suggesting 'no fat', but smaller amounts of fat for optimal health.

For more information on this topic contact: www.nyu.edu/education/nutrition

Steak & Oyster Pie

England

*W*e measure nutrients in grams. One gram is about the weight of one metal paperclip. One gram of protein or carbohydrate yields 4 calories, a gram of fat, 9 calories. For the same amount of weight, fat lends itself to more than twice the calories. Limiting fat is such an important part of the weight control/disease prevention process.

A good meat pie, made with a top and bottom butter pastry crust, is going to run close to 1000 calories and 52 grams of fat. No wonder it's so popular! So, is there any answer? I think I've got an 'upper crust' alternative. The crust is baked separately and married to the filling for five minutes before serving. This is a delicious and simple idea. This pie crust is almost fool proof. It has a good flavor, is crisp yet tender, and pairs beautifully with my crusted dishes. The only addition I'd make is a little mashed potato.

Main Dishes

Ingredients:

1/2 recipe Basic Pie Crust (see 'The Basics')
1 jar (10-ounces 284 g) medium oysters, drained, juice reserved, cut in 1" pieces
1 teaspoon non-aromatic olive oil, divided
1 medium onion, cut in 1" chunks
4 carrots, peeled, cut in half lengthwise, and sliced in 1/2" slices
1/2 pound turnips, peeled and cut in 1/2" chunks
3/4 pound medium mushrooms, halved (3 cups)
3/4 pound lean chuck steak, trimmed of all fat and cut in 1/2" chunks
2 heaping teaspoons tomato paste
2 cups canned or homemade low sodium beef stock (see 'The Basics')
1/4 teaspoon salt
1/8 teaspoon pepper
Bouquet Garni (see 'The Basics')
2 tablespoons arrowroot mixed with 1/4 cup beef broth or water (slurry)

Steak and Oyster Pie

1. Preheat the oven to 400°F (205°C). Make the whole pie crust recipe and freeze half for another use. Roll the crust into a 9" circle. Wrap it around your rolling pin and transfer to a baking sheet. Make a scalloped edge by pinching it all around with your fingers. Cut into 8 equal wedges and bake 10 minutes or until light gold and crisp. Set aside. Drain and chop the oysters, reserving the juice.

2. Heat 1/2 teaspoon of the oil in a high-sided skillet on medium high. Sauté the onions briskly to color for 2 to 3 minutes. Add the carrots, turnips and mushrooms and sauté 1 more minute. Turn out onto a plate.

3. Heat the remaining oil in the same skillet on high. Toss in the meat and brown on one side, 3 minutes. When it's nice and brown, stir in the tomato paste and cook until the paste darkens, 2 minutes. Add the vegetables to the meat; pour in the stock, oyster liquid, and salt and pepper. Add the bouquet garni, cover and simmer 1 1/2 hours or until the meat is tender.

4. Remove the bouquet garni. Stir in the slurry to thicken the sauce. Add the chopped oysters. Lay the cooked crust wedges on top and bake 5 minutes more before serving.

Serves 8

Nutrition and Disease Prevention

We are what we eat! The link between good nutrition and disease prevention has long been established by health care professionals but has not yet become part of our consciousness. We still seem to believe that what we eat has nothing to do with how we feel, beyond minor indigestion. Registered dietitians like Ann Gallagher, Former President of the American Dietetic Association, make it their job to educate us about the links between our diet and our health.

Ann Gallagher, RD
Former President, American Dietetic Association

What is a 'Registered Dietitian'?

Registered Dietitians are a preeminent source of nutrition information and are skilled at counseling individuals to make healthy diet and lifestyle changes. We teach people how to have good, healthy eating habits. A healthy diet, based on a variety of foods, can reduce the risk of many diseases — including heart disease, diabetes, and some forms of cancer.

How do you find a Registered Dietitian?

Dietitians are available in many professional settings, from private practices to hospital wards. Some Registered Dietitian's advertise in the yellow pages, but not too many. Contact your local outpatient clinic at the hospital and ask for a registered dietitian. Or in the United States, call The American Dietetic Association at 1-800-366-1655 or www.eatright.org.

What does a meeting with a Registered Dietitian involve?

* Creating a seven-day 'Food Diary' to reveal what you are eating on a regular basis (3-7 days).
* Discussing food likes and dislikes.
* Analyzing the food diary for nutritional adequacy.
* And making recommendations where and how changes can be made.

The result is an individualized meal plan with favorite foods included in moderation, so that long term behavior change can be maintained.

How can we measure moderation?

NUTRITIONAL PROFILE COMPARISON

Per serving	Nutrient Rich	Old Style
calories	276	918
fat (g)	12	52
saturated fat (g)	3	26
carbohydrates (g)	21	50
fiber (g)	2	2
sodium (mg)	257	1426

People feel better and have a lot more energy when they make improvements in their diet.

How can we measure moderation?

* Look at the Nutrition Facts food label, which discloses the portion size.
* Limit yourself to a single portion with each choice.
* Work with a Registered Dietitian to establish an individual calorie goal for yourself.
* Monitor your intake along with the assistance of a Registered Dietitian to better understand your individual needs.
* Measure foods that are unfamiliar to you so that you truly understand what an actual portion is.

For further information on this topic contact: www.eatright.org or call 1-800-366-1655 to find a registered dietitian in your area.

$\mathcal{M}$eatloaf

Calgary, Alberta

$\mathcal{W}$ork hard to be realistic with the weight management goals you set. Remember that any good thing does take time! Also remember to have a plan. When you are caught in an uncomfortable situation, it is so hard to make the right choice. By planning ahead you can work through your options and be primed to make a good choice. Hey guys, there is a sensible way to approach weight control and eating! Eat well, exercise regularly, and, most importantly, learn to be comfortable with yourself.

This has been quite a journey! Meatloaf can be a great example of 'anything-goes-just-as-long-as-it's-full-of-flavor'. Since fat is often full-of-flavor, it follows that most recipes contain ample provision. Early on in the search for great flavor without fat, I overdid the bread filling and the result was 'spongy'. This time around we've got it right. For a main dish or a sandwich, hot or cold, this hits the mark, with just 9 grams of fat per serving (compared to the Old Style 34 grams of fat per serving). Remember: when you lessen fat you must add taste, aroma, color and texture, hence the need for 18 ingredients. The sauce is the original invention from my New Zealand days and can be used with all manner of meat dishes from lamb chops to ribs. If you like ketchup and garlic, you'll love this!

Main Dishes

Ingredients:

Meat Loaf

1/2 teaspoon non-aromatic olive oil
1 cup finely chopped onion
2 cloves garlic, bashed and chopped
1 medium carrot, peeled and finely diced
 or grated (1/2 cup)
1/4 cup finely diced celery
1/2 cup finely diced red bell pepper
 (1/2 large)
1 teaspoon ground cumin
1 tablespoon mild chili powder
1/2 teaspoon allspice
1 teaspoon dried thyme
1-pound (450 g) extra lean (9% fat)
 ground beef
1-pound (450 g) extra lean ground turkey
1 tablespoon cocoa powder
1/2 cup ketchup
2/3 cup dry unseasoned bread crumbs
3/4 cup egg substitute
1/2 cup evaporated skim milk
1 teaspoon salt

Sauce

1/2 teaspoon non-aromatic olive oil
1 clove garlic, bashed and chopped
1 heaped tablespoon chopped parsley stems
1 cup ketchup
1 cup de-alcoholized dry white wine
1 tablespoon chopped parsley
1/4 cup water

Meatloaf

1. Preheat the oven to 350°F (180°C). Coat a large loaf pan with pan spray. Heat the oil in a small skillet on medium high. Sauté the onion 2 minutes, then add the garlic and continue cooking for 1 more minute. Stir in the carrot, celery, red pepper, cumin, chili powder, allspice, and thyme. Cook 4 minutes or until the vegetables are tender. Set aside to cool.

2. Place the ground beef, turkey, cocoa, ketchup, bread crumbs, egg substitute, milk, and salt in a large bowl. Add the sautéed vegetables and mix thoroughly. Tip into a large loaf pan and bake 1 hour and 15 minutes or until the internal temperature reaches 150°F. Let set 15 minutes to finish cooking before serving. As it sits the internal temperature will rise about 10°F to 160°F. (Meat must register at 160°F to kill bacteria.)

3. For the sauce, heat the oil in a small saucepan on medium high. Sauté the garlic and parsley stems 30 seconds. Add the ketchup and cook until it darkens and gets thick. Pour in the wine, parsley and water and simmer 5 minutes or until syrupy. Spoon over the slices of meat loaf or pass at the table.

The Psychology of Food

Whenever I'm away from home, Treena and I are always drawn to comfort foods like Roasted Chicken and Mashed Potatoes, or yes, even Meatloaf, though I usually order a child's portion! So it seemed an obvious connection that Dr Paul Garfinkel would discuss how to have a healthy view of food, and I would serve him my very 'new and improved' meatloaf that is carefully constructed to comfort without harm . . . surely a healthy 'psychological' view of food?

What does food mean to people?

* Food carries a fair amount of weight in people's minds because we do need it to survive — just like putting gas in the car, the body won't run without it. Food can also become a friend — an only friend to some — so it may be viewed as a comfort. Food can even be an escape, almost a lover of sorts as people look forward to time alone with food.

* The way we were raised and our culture affect the way we feel about food. Because of these factors, combined with the frequency with which we eat, eating habits are often difficult to break .

Paul Garfinkel, MD
Chief of Psychiatry, University of Toronto
President and CEO, Center for Addiction and Mental Health

What is body image and how are our images of the perfect body shaped by our culture?

* Thirty years ago body weight and ideal body image were close together, but in the last 30 years these two lines have grown farther apart. Society now views thinness as optimal, and as a result most people are unsatisfied with their bodies. This sets up an evaluative dynamic so that food is categorized as bad or evil.

* By age 12, body image is fixed in a young girl, but at 9 years of age you can affect their thinking and possibly prevent some of the problems that are a result of misunderstood body image (such as eating disorders).

What should be our goal in developing a healthy attitude towards food?

* Our primary goal is to reshape eating habits that may be resulting in unhealthy behaviors such as obesity or binge eating, and try to teach ways of gratification other than eating food. We need to develop a healthy relationship with our food.

NUTRITIONAL PROFILE COMPARISON

Per serving	Nutrient Rich	Old Style
calories	263	470
fat (g)	9	34
saturated fat (g)	3	14
carbohydrates (g)	20	14
fiber (g)	1	1
sodium (mg)	745	1036

* Our long-term goal should be to settle on a weight that is right for us genetically, then we should exercise, eat right — and be satisfied.

How do we develop a healthy view of food?

* Learn to reshape habits that may be resulting in unhealthy behaviors such as obesity or binge eating. For example, we can employ specific strategies to avoid over-eating when dining out: order small or appetizer size portions, halve an entrée with a friend, take half of the meal home. At parties have a snack before the party and be careful to limit your alcohol choices.

* Set small achievable goals that can be built upon to create success. It is very common to set unrealistic goals when you set out to make changes. We see diet books that say weight loss is easy, and images of perfect bodies have been created by unrealistic media exposure. If we don't accomplish our goals, then it is easy to be disappointed, which can lead to depression and then on to setting even more unrealistic goals or a desire to give up.

* Look at the portion size on the label, take that portion and put the rest back: this will help to set an attitude for trying to achieve moderation. Some people say that if you don't eat 'bad' foods, you will crave them and then overdo later. Some say you should stay away from these foods altogether and limit exposure to foods that give you problems. A qualified health professional can help you to assess what approach is best for you.

* The real key is to have a plan, know where you will be, what options you will have available so that you can make a good choice.

* Small amounts of weight loss can be great for our bodies — and for our minds. Recent findings in the Nurses Health Study, an impressive Harvard University study of over 100,000 nurses who have been followed for a long period of time, shows us that a small amount of weight loss (5 pounds) can make a tremendous difference in how people feel about themselves and spur them on to be even more successful with weight loss. This study shows how weight control empowers people.

For more information on this topic and additional resources contact: www.LearnEducation.com. In the United States call 1-800-736-7323, or in Canada call 1-817-545-4500.

Try to eliminate labeling foods 'good' or 'bad'. Instead aim for moderation, which should be defined as 'eating not too much or too little of a wide variety of foods.'

Three Sisters Stew

Washington, DC

.A.C.T. — *taste, aroma, color, texture. There is no reason why we should sacrifice any of these four elements of delicious food because we choose to prepare nutrient rich, low fat recipes. Another handy cooking acronym is F.A.B.I.S. — fresh and best in season. Cooking with F.A.B.I.S. foods will ensure 'fabulous' T.A.C.T. and good health!*

This could well be 'the' comfort food soup of the Americas. Not only are the ingredients seasonal but they also grow together in a complimentary way. The corn becomes the beanpole upon which the beans climb. The squash and peppers shade the soil and reduce weeds. They each give value to the other and are abundant. Fernando Divina discovered this real food of the Americas in his and his wife Marlene's search for dishes for their excellent Fiddleheads and Bella Coola Café in Portland, Oregon and for the restaurant in the Smithsonian Museum of the Americas in Washington, DC.

Ingredients:

Dumplings
scant 1/2 cup dry masa harina
1/3 cup water
1 teaspoon non-aromatic olive oil
2 tablespoons chopped cilantro
1/4 cup parmesan cheese
3/4 cup low fat cottage cheese
1/4 cup egg substitute or 1 whole egg

Stew
1 teaspoon non-aromatic olive oil
1 medium sweet onion, thinly sliced
2 cups fresh green beans, tipped, tailed,
  cut in 1" (2.5 cm) pieces
2 cups canned or homemade low
  sodium vegetable broth (see 'The Basics')
1 zucchini, cut in 1/2" (1.5 cm) chunks
1 15-ounce (425 g) can kidney beans, rinsed
  and drained
1 cup fresh, frozen or
  canned corn kernels
1/2 cup prepared green salsa
1/2 cup prepared red salsa
1 poblano chile, roasted, peeled and cut in
  1/2" (1.5 cm) pieces
2 Roma tomatoes, peeled and halved
1/4 cup chopped cilantro
roasted peppers (optional)

Three Sisters Stew

1. Combine the masa, water, oil, cilantro, parmesan cheese, cottage cheese, and egg substitute into a stiff dough. Set aside.

2. Heat the oil in a chef's pan or large saucepan on medium high. Sauté the onion until it begins to wilt, 2 minutes. Add the green beans and stock and simmer 5 minutes. Stir in the zucchini, kidney beans, corn, and green and red salsas.

3. Drop teaspoon size dumpling into the simmering soup and simmer 10 minutes more or until the dumplings are cooked and the green beans, tender. Stir in the chile pieces and tomato halves and heat through. Divide among 4 hot bowls and garnish with the chopped cilantro.

4. Add roasted peppers for additional intense flavor. Simply cut off the top and bottom of the pepper, cut a slit down one side of the pepper to remove the seed pod, and lay down flat in a nonstick pan on medium heat, cover and push down with a plate to roast. The pepper should be charred. By placing the hot pepper in plastic bag, the skin will come away from the pepper easily.

Serves 4

The Language of Flavor

What makes food flavorful? How do we taste what's bitter, sour, salty, sweet? Do we all 'taste the same'? These are some of the questions we posed to Professor Linda Bartoshuk from Yale University, an experimental psychologist who studies taste — tastefully, I might add. I found out, by the way, that I'm a 'supertaster', which accounts for my discomfort with highly spiced foods and bitter, unsweetened coffee.

How do we taste food?

Primarily with our tongues, but research has shown that there is no map of the tongue that includes salty and sour on the sides, bitter in the back, sweet on the front, as we used to think. Instead, everywhere that you have taste buds, you taste sweet, salty, sour, and bitter. Concerning aromas that accompany taste, there is a process called 'Retronasal Olfaction', which means that when the food is put in the mouth, chewing and swallowing pump the odors of the food up behind the palate into the nasal cavity.

Linda Bartoshuk, PhD
Professor, Department of Surgery (Otolaryngology) and Psychology, Yale University

What accounts for different tastes — like and dislikes? Why do some people seem more sensitive to flavors and aromas?

There are genetic variations in taste, with 'Non-Tasters' at one extreme and 'Super-Tasters' at the other. Non-Tasters have fewer fungiform papillae, which are the structures that contain the taste buds. Super-Tasters are capable of feeling two, three or four times as much pain as a Non-Taster. Super-Tasters are at greater health risk because they often eliminate bitter tasting foods (like Brussels Sprouts), which tend to have phytochemicals, and are often anti-cancer agents. Super-Tasters should consider eating these bitter foods by combining them with other ingredients to eliminate the bitter taste or by using alternative cooking methods that decrease bitterness.

What are some other common problems that people face with regard to taste?

We can experience 'phantoms' of any of the sensations perceived in the mouth. The term 'phantom' just means that we experience a sensation even though there is no obvious stimulus. The most common are taste phantoms and oral pain phantoms. Phantoms may result from damage to a nerve. At the site of damage the nerve generates a signal that is

NUTRITIONAL PROFILE COMPARISON

Per serving	Nutrient Rich	Old Style
calories	315	293
fat (g)	9	34
saturated fat (g)	3	14
carbohydrates (g)	47	31
fiber (g)	11	18
sodium (mg)	797	1650

transmitted to the brain and we experience sensations appropriate to the nerve that is damaged. You could think of this as 'pinching' a nerve. However, there is another way that phantoms can be caused: release of inhibition. The nerves in the mouth normally inhibit one another. Damage to one nerve releases some of that inhibition leading to sensations from other nerves.

What can happen to our taste when these nerves are damaged?

Taste from the front of the tongue, for example, normally inhibits taste on the rear of the tongue (opposite side). If we damage the taste nerve that goes to the front of the tongue on just one side, some people will experience 'taste phantoms' on the rear of the tongue on the opposite side.

Taste from the front of the tongue normally inhibits pain on the front of the tongue. If we damage the taste nerve going to the front of the tongue, some people will experience oral 'pain phantoms' on the front of the tongue. Supertasters are the most likely to experience these oral phantoms. We believe that the pain disorder called Burning Mouth Syndrome is an example of such an oral pain phantom. (Dr Miriam Grushka in Toronto is the world's expert on the treatment of this disorder.)

It is important to note that damage to nerves in the mouth alters oral sensations but does not lead to other disease.

For further information on this topic contact: www.tastelab.org

Learn what your taste preferences may be, then be creative in preparing recipes with foods that not only satisfy your personal taste but also provide foods from other taste groups to ensure good health.

ioppino
San Francisco, California

*A*s you plan meals, shop for groceries, and prepare food, include your children so that the 'gathering place' becomes a way to celebrate the whole family. At the same time, these kids will be learning the nutritional value of food. Not a bad combination — delicious food, good health, and a happy family!

It makes so much sense that this great seafood dish from Genoa, Italy should take its place among the splendid comfort foods of the San Francisco Bay area. The fishing fleets, agriculture, and the vineyards have all been blessed by Italian families who brought with them a robust and healthy regard for the flavors of home. In the Bay area, they found everything they needed to do justice to their long-established seafood 'casserole'. This is a perfect example of great flavor with lower risk. My only 'healthy' change in preparing this classic dish was to lower the oil content from 1/4 cup to 2 teaspoons.

Main Dishes

Ingredients:

Sauce

2 teaspoons non-aromatic olive oil
1 large sweet onion, chopped in 1" dice
6 cloves garlic, bashed and chopped
  (2 tablespoons)
1 large red bell pepper, cut in 1" dice
1 12-ounce can tomato puree
6 Roma tomatoes, peeled, seeded
  and chopped
2 cups de-alcoholized dry white wine
5 parsley stems, tied together
1 teaspoon dried oregano
1 teaspoon dried basil
1 teaspoon dried thyme

Fish

18 small clams, scrubbed
18 small mussels, scrubbed and bearded
1 dungeness crab, cooked
1 pound halibut steaks, cut in 1 1/2" chunks
18 medium shrimp (21/30 per pound),
  peeled and de-veined

Garnish

1/2 cup chopped parsley

Cioppino

1. Heat oil in a 10" (25 cm) chef's pan on medium high. Sauté the onion for 3 minutes or until translucent but not browned. Add the garlic and red pepper and sauté 3 minutes more. Stir in the tomato puree, chopped tomatoes and white wine. Season with the parsley stems, oregano, basil and thyme. Simmer 25 minutes.

2. Prepare the fish. Bring 1/2 cup water to a boil in a chef's pan or skillet with a lid. Toss in the clams and mussels. Cover and cook 3 minutes or until they open, discarding the ones that remain closed. Drain and set aside. Break the crab in half through the thin part of the body. You will have 2 body halves with the legs and claws attached. Now separate the legs and claws so each one has a body segment attached. Set aside.

3. Gently stir in the halibut chunks and simmer 4 minutes. Add the shrimp, crab, clams, and mussels and continue to simmer 8 minutes. Remove parsley stems. Stir in chopped parsley and serve in bowls with a slice of good hearty Italian bread.

Serves 6

Celebrating the Family

We invited Chef David St John-Grubb and Registered Dietitian Cathy Powers to The Gathering Place to explore the importance of making time for the family while preparing food and dining at the table. To include our children in our plans for eating well for good health may seem an obvious thing to do, but this is not always easy in our fast-paced, fast-food world. What we do at the table in teaching them nutritional and family values may last them a 'long' lifetime.

How can we get kids into the kitchen, willingly?

We see at least four ways to get kids into the kitchen and gathered around the table:

1. Make sure everybody participates in planning meals and going to the grocery store together.

2. Let kids help in preparing the meal, chopping, dicing, stirring. Join them in setting the table attractively, even playfully.

3. Maintain a well-stocked pantry so that stocks, grains, spices, and other basic ingredients based on your family's preferences are all readily available.

4. Prepare 'Speed Scratch' meals so that food can be on the table in a short amount of time — a graham cracker crumb prepared, pasta fresh or frozen available, pizza dough ready to roll.

Be sure to establish planning, shopping, preparation, and dining routines — and stick to them. Make gathering around the table at dinner time a priority in your family life.

What are the benefits of bringing children to the table?

They get to experience the peace of being part of a family and find comfort in dinner conversation. Parents can learn what their children are doing through the freedom of expression that dinner conversation encourages. You can ask what your kids did that day and develop a one-on-one conversation. The table can also be a place to talk through problems so children don't have to resolve problems on their own. And we can

David St. John-Grubb,
MCFA (CG), CMC, CECCHE, MHCIMA

Cathy Powers, MS, RD

NUTRITIONAL PROFILE COMPARISON

Per serving	Nutrient Rich	Old Style
calories	271	271
fat (g)	5	25
saturated fat (g)	1	3
carbohydrates (g)	20	12
fiber (g)	4	2
sodium (mg)	496	729

teach them the basics of good nutrition so that they will come to know and enjoy the difference between a meal rich in fruits and vegetables and a fast-food meal that will often lack nutrition.

For further information on this topic contact: www.foodworks-intl.com and www.eatright.org

Explore ways of bringing your children to the family 'table' by involving them in meal planning, grocery shopping, and food preparation.

Scottish Irish Stew
Scotland

Treena and I have successfully experimented with limiting the 'processed' carbohydrates in our diet, striving for a 50% drop in refined carbohydrates such as cakes and cookies and a decrease in complex carbohydrates like pasta and bread that are often served in super-size portions. We don't ban or 'demonize' these foods but instead focus on limiting our portion sizes, resulting in fewer calories and better health.

I am extremely fond of this dish. If you want to know what can always comfort me, it's found right here. The sweet taste of lamb that is simmered on-the-bone, the succulence of the simple vegetables, the smooth delicacy of barley, and my completely new idea of serving it upon a thick bed of raw leaf spinach (that partially wilts under the sauce). Well . . . it's delicious!

Main Dishes

Ingredients:

Stew Base

1 teaspoon non-aromatic olive oil
1 medium onion, coarsely chopped
5 cups canned or homemade low sodium
  chicken stock (see 'The Basics'), divided
1 1/4 pounds lamb necks

Stew

1/4 cup barley (this can be increased to
  1/2 cup)
4 medium carrots, peeled and cut into
  1/2" (1.5 cm) pieces
1 pound yellow potatoes, peeled and cut into
  1/2" (1.5 cm) pieces
18 small boiling onions, peeled
1/2 teaspoon black pepper
1/4 teaspoon salt
18 whole white mushrooms,
  to match onion size
1 pound fresh spinach leaves, washed and
  stemmed

Scottish Irish Stew

1. To make the stew base, heat the oil in a high-sided skillet on medium. Sauté the onions 1 minute. Add 4 cups of the stock and the lamb necks and bring to a boil. Reduce the heat and simmer, covered, 2 1/2 hours or until the meat falls off the bone. When the lamb is cooked, remove from broth and separate the meat from the bones. Reserve the meat and discard the bones. Strain the broth into a fat separator.

2. To make the stew, return the de-fatted broth to the pan and pour in the remaining cup of chicken broth. Now add the barley, carrots, potatoes, onions, pepper and salt. Simmer, covered, on medium low for 30 minutes. Add the mushrooms and reserved meat and cook 5 more minutes.

3. Line 6 bowls with raw spinach leaves, pointed end up. Ladle the stew into the lined bowls and serve.

Serves 6

Vegetarian Option: Scottish Irish Stew

1. Peel 1 pound parsnips and cut into 2" pieces. Sprinkle with 2 tablespoons tamari and let set for 15 minutes.

2. Heat 1 teaspoon non-aromatic olive oil in a high sided skillet, sauté the parsnips, carrots, potatoes, onions and 2 turnips, peeled and cut into 1/2" pieces, 2 minutes. Add 1/2 cup barley, and pepper and pour in 5 cups low sodium vegetable broth. (Leave the salt out as the tamari is very salty.) Bring to a boil, reduce the heat, and simmer 30 minutes. Stir in the mushrooms and cook 5 minutes more.

3. Serve in spinach lined bowls as in step 3 above.

Food Portions

A *national survey on weight gain in the 1980s found that people had gained on average 8 pounds per person in just one decade. Many more people were obese in 1990 than in 1980. While there is no one explanation for this remarkable change in the 'national' weight, one cause is an increase in portion sizes at home and in restaurants. Registered Dietitian Lisa R. Young explains the relationship between portion size and obesity.*

Lisa R. Young, MS, RD, CDN
Doctoral Student, Department of Nutrition and Food Studies, New York University

What are the issues with regard to portion sizes?

People underestimate the food portions that they eat on a daily basis by up to 50%, we have discovered during diet consultations, for several reasons:

* Portion sizes are variable within food categories. Breads are most confusing where 1 serving = 1 slice of bread, 1/2 cup of pasta, or 1 pretzel.

* Portions may be sized differently depending on where you dine. For example, many bagels can be up to 5 bread servings (1 oz. = 1 serving). A 'ballgame' pretzel is 5 bread servings. Most muffins are 5 or 6 bread servings, not to mention the fat content!

* When food is served as part of a meal, it is hard to conceptualize the serving size. One pasta dish in a restaurant can yield at least 1,000 calories, and is often tossed with vegetables, meat, and added fats like oil or butter.

What can we do to take control of portion sizes?

1. Learn about standard portions so that you can make a better assessment of your food choices. See a registered dietitian to counsel you on accurate and appropriate portion sizes and to help you assess what you are currently doing and how you can improve.

2. Think of handy ways to measure portion sizes. For example, think of a 3 oz. meat portion as similar to a deck of cards or the size and thickness of a woman's palm.

3. Plan ahead for meals — a steak moderately portioned is okay if you focus on grains, vegetables, fruits the rest of the day.

4. Buy smaller single serving bags of chips and snacks because when people buy a larger portion they generally eat it.

NUTRITIONAL PROFILE COMPARISON

Per serving	Nutrient Rich	Vegetarian	Old Style
calories	277	273	662
fat (g)	6	2	18
saturated fat (g)	2	0	6
carbohydrates (g)	35	59	48
fiber (g)	13	18	6
sodium (mg)	211	200	615

5. In restaurants, split meals (especially the meat portion) and add more vegetables, salads, or side dishes. Order appetizer portions, a salad and a soup, or take half of your meal home in a 'doggie' bag. Tell the waiter you're trying to live within reason and ask if the chef can prepare smaller portions.

For more information on these and other important nutrition issues: Call 1-800-366-1655 or visit www.eatright.org

To manage our weight, we need to understand portion sizes and reduce them if needed.

⸿ottage Pie

England

What is a healthy weight for you? Here is a 'general' guideline. For women, allow 100 pounds for the first five feet, and for every inch over five feet, add five pounds. For men, allow 106 pounds for the first five feet, adding six pounds for every inch over five feet. Add 10% for a large frame, subtract 10% for a small frame. Remember that each one of us has many individuals needs, so before you panic, consult a health care professional to identify a target weight for you!

Treena and I have had 27 homes since we married in 1955. Contrary to popular belief, I'm not an Aussie or a Kiwi, although we loved our 9 years 'down under'. We started in England. This dish is about as English as you can get. As with any popular dish of the people it can be made very differently. This one was created for my mother Mardi's 90th birthday in lieu of a cake. She wanted her nurses to get a real 'taste of my home'. The basic method works well for all kinds of savory minced meats.

Main Dishes

Ingredients:

3 cups canned or homemade low sodium
  beef stock (see 'The Basics'), divided
1/4 cup bulgur wheat
1 teaspoon non-aromatic olive oil, divided
12 ounces extra lean (9%) ground beef
3 tablespoons tomato paste
1 1/2 cups chopped onion
2 cloves garlic, bashed and chopped
1 cup finely chopped carrots
1/4 cup finely chopped celery
1 teaspoon dried thyme
1 tablespoon Worcestershire sauce
4 teaspoons arrowroot or cornstarch mixed
  with 2 tablespoons beef stock (slurry)
1/4 teaspoon salt
1 recipe mashed potatoes
1 tablespoon chopped fresh parsley

Ingredients: Vegetarian Option

Replace the beef broth with vegetable broth, the bulgur with 1/2 cup of barley, the beef with 3/4 pounds of chopped portobello mushrooms, and the Worcestershire sauce with tamari or soy sauce.

Cottage Pie

1. Preheat the oven to 350°F (180°C). Heat the beef stock and pour 2 cups over the bulgur wheat. Set aside for at least 10 minutes to soften.

2. Heat a high-sided skillet on high until very hot. Add 1/2 teaspoon of the oil, break the beef up into small spoon sized pieces and add to the pan to brown. Mash the meat down so it crumbles after it has browned. Reduce the heat, stir in the tomato paste, and cook until the paste turns dark red. Pour in the remaining cup of beef stock and stir to release any flavorful bits left on the bottom of the pan. Pour into a bowl and set aside.

3. Without washing the pan, heat the remaining 1/2 teaspoon of oil on medium high and sauté the onions. After 2 minutes, add the garlic, carrots, celery, and thyme. Continue cooking for 2 more minutes. Add the Worcestershire sauce, softened bulgur with its stock, and cooked meat. Simmer 10 minutes or until the carrots are tender. Stir in the slurry to thicken, and then taste for salt.

4. Cover the filling with mashed potatoes; one spoon full at a time makes it easier. Make attractive designs on top with a fork. Bake in the preheated oven for 20 minutes to heat through. Turn on the broiler to brown the top for 2 to 3 minutes. Sprinkle the top with parsley and cut into 6 wedges. A classic vegetable side dish would be peas cooked with a little mint and perhaps a broiled tomato.

Serves 6

Vegetarian Option: Barley Mushroom Cottage Pie

1. Heat the high-sided skillet with the oil. Cook the onions for 2 minutes, add the garlic, celery, and thyme and cook 1 minute more. Add chopped portobello mushrooms and cook until they give up their water, 5 minutes. Stir in the tomato paste, cooking until the vegetables are coated and the paste darkens.

2. Pour in the vegetable broth and barley. Cover and cook at a slow boil for 15 minutes. Add the carrots and tamari and cook 15 more minutes. Continue with step 4 above.

Tailored Cookbooks

Here's another great 'hoffen-ing'. Professor Vic Strecher and his charming daughter Julia came to The Gathering Place to discuss the value of creating your own cookbook, collecting family favorites which attend not only to personal likes and dislikes but also to everyone's nutritional needs. By tailoring a family eating plan, we can prepare foods everyone enjoys and prevent disease before it starts. I hope some of my recipes find their way into your tailored cookbook!

How do we go about developing a cookbook that is tailored to our family's likes and needs?

* We need to collect information from individual family members on their food preferences and their nutritional needs.

* At a center like Health Research Labs in Michigan, this information can be analyzed by health care professionals using a computer program to generate a highly tailored recipe plan.

* Qualified health professionals can also determine barriers to making positive behavior change so that these can be addressed as part of the eating plan.

What are the benefits of a tailored cookbook?

* People can more easily reduce fat in their diet with tailored information.

* Recipes can be tailored to meet a whole families needs.

* Time constraints and skill level of the individual will be determined and figured into the tailored cookbook.

For further information on this topic contact: www.healthmedia.net

Vic Strecher, MD, MPH
Director, Health Media Inc.
Professor, Health Media Research Labs,
University of Michigan

NUTRITIONAL PROFILE COMPARISON

Per serving	Nutrient Rich	Vegetarian	Old Style
calories	386	220	597
fat (g)	11	3	32
saturated fat (g)	4	0	13
carbohydrates (g)	53	4	36
fiber (g)	6	4	4
sodium (mg)	433	448	539

Tailored cookbooks can help people to prevent disease before it starts.

Jerk Marinated Lamb Stew
Toronto, Ontario

Digest these facts! Our digestive system, spread out, covers almost the length of a football field. Among nutrients, carbohydrates are easiest to digest, proteins take a little longer than carbohydrates, and fats take the longest. By reducing fat in your diet, you may not only enhance the health of your heart but you might also give your stomach a break!

Toronto may seen like a long haul from Jamaica, especially in a long hard winter, but wait for summer and then celebrate with the Caribbean people who are very much at home in this, the second most culturally diverse city on earth. (London UK is #1) The traditional jerk seasoning has become a worldwide favorite. I worked on a milder version of a lamb stew that you can upgrade to make the title 'jerk' seem almost motionless.

Main Dishes

Ingredients:

1 teaspoon non-aromatic olive oil, divided
2 scallions, chopped
2 large cloves garlic, bashed and chopped
1 1/2 tablespoons allspice berries, crushed
  or 1/2 teaspoon ground allspice
1/2 teaspoon crushed chilies
  (increase for heat)
1 teaspoon thyme
2" (5 cm) ginger root cut in slices
2 cups + 2 tablespoons dealcoholized
  red wine, divided
1/2 teaspoon + 1/8 teaspoon salt
1 1/2 pounds (675 g) lean lamb leg cut in
  1" (2.5 cm) chunks
18 pearl onions, peeled or 1 can pearl onions
1 pound baby carrots
1 bunch collard greens, washed and
  stemmed
1/8 teaspoon ground cayenne pepper
  (increase for heat)
1 tablespoon arrowroot mixed with 2 tablespoons dealcoholized red wine or water
  (slurry)

Jerk Marinated Lamb Stew

1. Heat 1/2 teaspoon of the oil in a chef's pan or high-sided skillet on medium high. Add the scallions, garlic, allspice, chiles, thyme, and ginger. Cook, stirring, 2 minutes. Pour in 1 cup of the wine and 1/2 teaspoon of the salt and continue cooking until the wine is almost gone, 5 minutes. Strain into a bowl and rinse the pan with the other cup of wine and add to the bowl. Pour over the meat and marinate 8 hours or overnight. The marinade is used to denature proteins on the outside of the meat, softening the meat and adding flavor, while infiltrating the top of the meat to give a 'tingling' in the back of your throat. Drain, reserving the marinade, and pat dry.

2. Preheat the oven to 350°F (180°C). Heat the remaining oil in a chef's pan or high-sided skillet on high. Drop in the meat in one layer and do not disturb until browned on one side, 2-3 minutes. (You can peek as you start to see the bottom browning around the edges.) Tip the meat onto a plate and add the onions and carrots to the hot pan. Cook, stirring, 3 or 4 minutes or until they start to brown just a little. Pour the reserved marinade over the top and let it boil. Return the meat with any accumulated juices to the pan. Pour the reserved marinade over the top, cover and bake in the preheated oven 1 hour.

3. Remove the pan from the oven. Drop the collard greens into the pan, sprinkle with the ground red pepper and remaining salt and cover 5 minutes. Cook 5 minutes over medium heat. Remove to the plate with the meat and other vegetables, starting with a good layer of the collard greens. Thicken the remaining liquid with the slurry. Pour the sauce over the meat and vegetables and serve.

Serves 6

Digestion Facts

Did you know that 92% of what we eat will be digested by the body (99% of all protein is digested and 97% of fat)? Registered dietitian Deanna L. Miller brought these and other facts to the show for us to 'digest' along with a long list of helpful hints for improving digestion and improving our health.

What is our most common digestive problem?

Over 60 million Americans suffer from 'heartburn' at least once a month. Food is regurgitated back up into the esophagus because we may eat too fast, swallow too much air while eating, or eat an incompatible variety of foods.

How can we avoid heartburn?

* Lower fat in our diet.
* Eat more fruits and vegetables.
* Eat more fiber and drink more water.
* Choose healthy foods on a regular basis (3 meals a day) and be consistent.
* Avoid certain foods which may cause digestive problems for some individuals: caffeine, chocolate, peppermint, and alcohol (these foods can weaken the muscle in the esophagus).
* Limit milk since it promotes acid secretion.
* Use antacids when necessary and stay in contact with your personal physician who can monitor your health.

What other suggestions do you have for improving digestion?

The speed at which you eat is important. It takes 20 minutes for the brain to signal the stomach to tell it that it is full, so if you eat fast, you may overeat because you won't feel full. This leads to:

1. eating too much

2. heartburn

3. weight gain and obesity

Deanna L. Miller, RD
Oropharyngeal Coordinator,
Missouri Baptist Medical Center

NUTRITIONAL PROFILE COMPARISON

Per serving	Nutrient Rich	Old Style
calories	317	745
fat (g)	12	43
saturated fat (g)	4	17
carbohydrates (g)	15	14
fiber (g)	3	5
sodium (mg)	380	874

So, slow down at your next meal. Here's how:

4. Put your fork or spoon down between each bite.

5. Start talking more at dinner.

6. Drink more water, which will aid your digestion and just might help you to eat less. You need to drink up 8-10 cups of liquid daily, ideally water and juices for optimal digestion (but not coffee, cola, or caffeinated beverages).

7. Chew food a given number of times.

8. Limit portions.

For more information on these and other important nutrition issues: Call 1-800-366-1655 or visit www.eatright.org

Petite Coq au Vin

Montreal, Quebec

Eat less, move more — that's the very best weight loss program that the world has to offer until the magic 'calorie burner' pill is perfected. When it arrives, it may easily challenge Viagra for top spot among the 'celebrity' pharmaceuticals! Still, I shall continue to eat less and move more because it feels so good.

A chicken cooked gently in red wine, now what could be more French . . . or more delicious? I took this classic and used the Rock Cornish game hens, the small flavorful North American bi-partisan or multi-national experiment in genetics and bathed it in a Napa Valley Cabernet Sauvignon (with it's alcohol removed by reverse osmosis . . . which leaves the original wine flavors intact). Add new potatoes to the 'casserole' and spinach as a side dish and you'll get more than a 'whiff' of the pleasures in store for you at the French flavored tables of Quebec.

Main Dishes

Ingredients:

1/2 teaspoon olive oil

2 Rock Cornish game hens (24 oz, 680 g each) cut in half

10 ounces (284 g) pearl onions, peeled

3 ounces (85 g) Canadian bacon, cut in 1/2" pieces

2 medium turnips, peeled and cut in 1" pieces

12 medium mushrooms, whole

1 pound (454 g) tiny new potatoes, whole with skin

1/2 teaspoon dried thyme

1/4 teaspoon salt

1/4 teaspoon pepper

3 bay leaves

1 1/2 cups canned or homemade low sodium chicken stock (see 'The Basics')

1 1/2 cups de-alcoholized red wine

2 tablespoons arrowroot mixed with 4 tablespoons water (slurry)

1 pound spinach leaves, washed and stemmed

2 tablespoons chopped fresh parsley

Petite Coq au Vin

1. Preheat the oven to 350°F (180°C). Heat the oil in a 10 1/2" (26.5 cm) chef's pan on medium-high. Brown the hens skin side down, turning once, 5 minutes. It will be a tight squeeze, but no matter. Remove from the pan and set aside.

2. Place the onions, Canadian bacon, turnips, mushrooms, potatoes, and thyme into the pan and cook, stirring, 2 or 3 minutes. Add the salt, pepper, bay leaves and pour in the stock and wine. Return the browned hens to the pan, cover, and bring to a boil. Bake in the preheated oven for 40 minutes.

3. Remove the chicken to a plate to cool slightly, before removing the skin and bones. Leave the flesh in the largest pieces possible. Discard the skin bones and bay leaves. Carefully strain the liquid into a fat strainer then pour back into the pan (through a sieve) without the fat. Bring to a boil and let it boil, uncovered, 10 minutes to reduce the liquid and finish the vegetables.

4. Stir in the slurry and return the cooked chicken. Heat until thickened. Place a handful of raw spinach leaves into each of 6 bowls and ladle the stew over the top. Sprinkle parsley on each serving.

Serves 6

Special Techniques:

* Blanche small onions to remove outer skin, drop in boiling water for two or three minutes and when removed, the skin will slip right off.

Fidget Factor

We invited Professor Victor Katch back to The Gathering Place to tell us more about the 'fidget factor', which he discusses at greater length in his book of the same title. We don't necessarily need to plan elaborate exercise programs to lose weight — we just need to move around more. Just watch me 'fidget' while I'm cooking!

What is the cumulative effect of calorie expenditure or exercise on weight control?

Here are some 'Fidget Facts':

1. Very small changes in our behavior for a long period of time will add up and often result in weight loss. For example, consistently taking the stairs rather than the elevator could mean a 3 pound weight loss in a year.

2. You can lose 8 pounds a year by just 'fidgeting' around at work or at home. Your goal is to be more physically active whenever you can.

3. You just need to get active! Exercise specific devices, like machines that exercise just one part of the body, are probably less effective than whole body exercises. If your goal is calorie expenditure, whatever will help you to exercise regularly is best.

For general health and weight control most individuals should expend about 300 calories through exercise each day. This would be equivalent to moving about three miles a day. The exercise doesn't have to be done all at the same time. Most people walk at a rate of 18-20 minutes a mile, so about 45 minutes of continuous, non-stop movement would result in a 300 calorie deficit.

For more information on this topic contact: The Division of Kinesiology, University of Michigan, at www.umich.edu

Victor L. Katch, PhD
Professor, Kinesiology, University of Michigan
Author, *The Fidget Factor* and *Exercise Physiology: Energy, Nutrition and Human Performance*

NUTRITIONAL PROFILE COMPARISON

Per serving	Nutrient Rich	Old Style
calories	316	766
fat (g)	7	44
saturated fat (g)	2	17
carbohydrates (g)	31	13
fiber (g)	9	2
sodium (mg)	707	1257

Yankee Pot Roast
with Horseradish Mashed Potatoes
New Hampshire

When some people become so fat 'phobic' that they eliminate red meat from their diet, they may eliminate a really important source of iron, a mineral necessary for good health. For most of us, lean red meat can be eaten occasionally if consumed in appropriately sized portions.

Of course other nations had already used the same method of pot roasting to gain succulent tenderness from otherwise 'tough cuts' of beef, but somehow the appellation 'Yankee' to pot roast has not only stuck, but goes almost as far as apple pie to express the pure pleasure of American family life around a fall or winter table (never ever to be replaced by take out pizza and television . . . please, never!) I tested rump roast against the often used chuck roast and found it easier to cut across the grain and eventually (after 3 hours) just as tender as the 2 1/2 hour chuck. It pays to ask your butcher for a rump piece that will easily cut across the grain. I prefer to use cider vinegar rather than red wine, feeling that it separates the recipe from its French counterpart. We serve a 3-4 ounce meat portion, at 390 calories and 8 grams of fat, against the classic 6-7 ounces, which registers at 903 calories and 53 grams of fat, thereby, in part, cutting out over 500 calories. Wow!

Main Dishes

Ingredients:

Yankee Pot Roast

1 teaspoon non-aromatic olive oil, divided
1 onion, chopped
3 tablespoons tomato paste
2 carrots, chopped
2 ribs celery, chopped
2 1/2 pounds beef rump roast
3 1/2 cups canned or homemade low sodium
  beef stock (see 'The Basics')
3/4 teaspoon salt, divided
2 tablespoons cider vinegar
6 medium carrots, peeled and roll cut
  or cut on the diagonal in 1" pieces
2 small turnips, peeled and cut in 1" chunks
18 whole medium mushrooms
18 pearl onions, blanched 3 minutes in
  boiling water and peeled
4 tablespoons arrowroot mixed
  with 1/2 cup water (slurry)
2 tablespoons chopped parsley
Bouquet Garni (see 'The Basics')

Horseradish Mashed Potatoes

3 pounds Russet potatoes,
  peeled and quartered
1/2 cup buttermilk
1/4 teaspoon salt
1 tablespoon horseradish

Yankee Pot Roast
with Horseradish Mashed Potatoes

1. Heat 1/2 teaspoon of the oil in a Dutch oven on medium high. Sauté the onions 3 minutes, then add the tomato paste, stirring until it darkens, about 6 more minutes. Add the chopped carrots and celery and mix to coat with the tomato paste. Remove to a plate and without washing the pan, return it to the heat. Put the remaining oil on a large plate and add 1/4 teaspoon each salt and pepper. Rub the meat on all sides ready for the hot pan. Drop the roast into the hot pan and brown on all sides. This will happen quickly because of the residual tomato paste in the pan, about 4 minutes. Remove the meat to the plate with the vegetables.

2. Pour some of the stock into the pan and scrape up all the browned bits stuck to the bottom. Return the vegetables and top with the meat. Pour the rest of the stock into the pan along with 1/2 teaspoon of the salt and the vinegar. Drop the bouquet garni into the stock, cover and bring to a boil. Reduce the heat and simmer 3 hours or until the meat is fork tender. Cook the carrots and turnips together in a saucepan with a little water and the remaining 1/4 teaspoon salt for ten minutes. Drain and set aside.

3. Remove the roast to a plate and cover to keep warm. Pour the cooking liquid through a sieve into a fat strainer; discard the tired old vegetables and the herb bundle. Pour the defatted juices back into the pan. Bring to a boil and add the mushrooms, partially cooked onions, and the reserved carrots and turnips. Cook until just heated through, 3 or 4 minutes. Stir in the slurry and heat to thicken.

4. While the vegetables are heating, cut the meat into 1/4" (.75 cm) slices across the grain. Lay the slices on a hot plate and spoon some of the sauce over the top. Serve the vegetables, mashed potatoes, and gravy family style in separate serving dishes.

Serves 8

Horseradish Mashed Potatoes

1. Boil the potatoes until very soft, about 20 minutes. Drain, cover with a clean dishtowel and leave on the stove with the heat off for 5 minutes or until thoroughly dried out and floury on top.

2. Mash and stir in buttermilk, salt and horseradish to taste and consistency preference.

Iron Clad Nutrition

From the author of Stealth Health, Evelyn Tribole, we learned that the single most deficient nutrient in diets worldwide is iron. While we might be tempted to chew nails to meet our dietary need for iron, eating iron rich foods might be more flavorful— and easier on the teeth! We discussed various ways to incorporate this critical mineral into our daily diet.

Evelyn Tribole, MS, RD
Nutrition Consultant and Author, *Stealth Health*

What is the function of iron in our bodies?

* Located in every red blood cell, iron holds onto oxygen and that is what gives us energy.
* Iron is involved in many enzyme systems throughout our body and helps to build a strong immune system.
* Iron helps with the thinking process. If children do not get enough iron, they will often have behavioral, irritability, and thought problems.
* Iron aids in the removal of fat from the blood.

How much iron do we need?

An adult male and children aged 1 to 10 have the same iron requirement of 10 milligrams of iron daily, while most women need 15 milligrams. Iron requirements during pregnancy increase significantly.

What are some symptoms of iron deficiency or anemia (a.k.a. iron poor blood)?

* Persistent fatigue. We feel tired for days on end.
* Behavioral and thought problems. Children, for example, may have trouble learning.
* Often feel cold. We can't seem to get warm.
* Problems sleeping at night.

Iron deficiency can be revealed in a simple blood test, so check with your physician if you think you are deficient in iron.

What are the best sources of iron?

* Food sources include red meat and the dark meat of chicken and turkey are best.

NUTRITIONAL PROFILE COMPARISON

Per serving	Nutrient Rich	Old Style
calories	390	903
fat (g)	8	53
saturated fat (g)	3	21
carbohydrates (g)	43	57
fiber (g)	6	8
sodium (mg)	452	891

* Other foods can increase absorption of the iron you are eating. For example, combining vitamin C-rich foods, like orange juice, broccoli, peppers, and strawberries, with foods containing iron can increase the iron absorption up to 85% more than if you eat iron-rich foods on their own.

* Cooking food in an iron skillet or a stainless steel pan will increase the amount of iron in a dish as well. Incidentally, minerals like iron cannot be 'overcooked'.

* Tea and coffee can inhibit the iron absorption.

* Iron supplements taken with calcium supplements will not be absorbed as well, so the supplements should be taken at different times of the day.

* Iron can be consumed in excess, so don't overdue the supplements; always check with you physician and/or a registered dietitian about your individual requirements.

For further information on this topic contact: www.eatright.org, call 1-800-366-1655, or read Evelyn's book, *Stealth Health*.

ea Sea Pie
Mt Vernon, Washington

I'm always visiting local farmer's markets, trying to find F.A.B.I.S. foods (fresh and best in season) in order to make the best regional dishes. It seems obvious to me that all the old 'classics' came about because practically everything was locally grown in the one season. Cooking with fresh, seasonal foods also supports our local farmers who are our culinary 'kin'.

Now, I happen to live in the middle of one of the greatest green pea harvesting centers in the world, the Skagit Valley, which fits pretty well halfway between Vancouver, British Columbia and Seattle, Washington. The main township is Mount Vernon. There is no 'classic' dish in our history, so why not start one? We looked around and found potatoes, basil, dill, parsley, sweet onions (fairly local from Walla Walla), garlic, salmon, and, of course . . . peas. With this we've made a special bakers pie (one that used to be baked with one's neighbors in the baker's oven after the last of the loaves were done). It's a simple seafood and potato pie, but wow . . . when it's launched on a pea green sea . . . watch out!

Main Dishes

Ingredients:

2 pounds (900 g) medium red potatoes
14-ounce (340 g) fresh salmon fillet
1 generous tablespoon chopped fresh basil
1 generous tablespoon chopped fresh dill
1 generous tablespoon chopped fresh parsley
1 teaspoon non-aromatic olive oil
1/2 large sweet onion, sliced (generous cup)
3 cloves garlic, bashed and chopped
    (1 tablespoon)
2 1/2 cups low sodium fish or chicken stock,
    divided
2 tablespoons arrowroot mixed with
    1/4 cup stock or water (slurry)
1/4 teaspoon freshly ground
    black pepper
3 tablespoons freshly grated Parmesan cheese
1-pound (450 g) frozen petite peas, thawed
1/4 teaspoon salt

Pea Sea Pie

1. Steam the potatoes whole for 20 minutes or until they fall off a knife stuck into the middle. Cool, peel and slice about 1/8 inch thick. Cut thin slices of the salmon across the fillet on the diagonal from the top down to the skin. Discard the skin. Combine the chopped herbs and divide in half. Coat an 8″ x 8″ (20 x 20 cm) baking dish with pan spray. Preheat the oven to 350°F (180°C).

2. Heat the oil in a chef's pan on medium high. Sauté the onions until they start to turn translucent, 3 minutes. Add the garlic and cook 2 minutes more. Pour in 2 cups of the stock and bring to a boil. Thicken with the slurry and set aside.

3. Lay half of the potato slices (use the uneven end pieces here) on the bottom of the baking dish. You will use half the herbs to assemble the dish. Sprinkle with herbs and pepper, then lay half the salmon slices on top of the potatoes. Add more herbs and pepper. Now layer the rest of the salmon on top and scatter with more herbs, pepper and the onions from the sauce. Top with the remaining potatoes in an attractive pattern and a little more of the mixed herbs. Pour the sauce over the top. Sprinkle with the cheese and bake in the preheated oven for 15 minutes.

4. Reserve 1 cup of the peas for garnish. Whiz the rest with the remaining stock in a blender until very smooth, 2 minutes. Press the puree through a sieve. When the pie is done, cut in 4 pieces. Strain the remaining juice into the sauce, using a suitably sized plate, held firmly in place with cloth. Add the salt, the remaining fresh herbs, and the whole peas. Heat until steam starts to come off the top of the sauce. You want to preserve the color of the peas, which is threatened by heat. Pour the sauce in a puddle to cover the place, and then serve your potato islands on the pea green sea!

Serves 4

Special Techniques:

* To keep chopped herbs looking fresh, spray them lightly with a spray oil, which will coat them and prevent them from discoloring.

Farmers' Markets

The 'hoffen-ing' Gail Feenstra brought to our show was the idea of 'Community Supported Agriculture' (CSA) where people buy shares in local market farms that pay 'dividends' in fresh food in season. As the produce is harvested, the shareholders come by to pick up their weekly supply of fresh, locally grown fruits, vegetables, herbs, and flowers. And the farmers have new capital to 'grow' their farms. It works well for all concerned!

What are the benefits of buying food from local farmers' markets?

* Farmers who come together to market their produce and other products directly to consumers not only offer fresh fruits and vegetables indigenous to the region but sometimes they make value-added products like flavored oils and dried fruits and vegetables.

* In-season foods are typically higher in nutrient value because they are fresh — and they taste better, too.

* When we know from whom we are buying our food, we can develop a relationship with the farmer (relational shopping) which adds a personal 'value' to the food.

* Buying directly from the farmer can eliminate the 'middleman' and provide us with a great sense of helping the farmers make their living. This way we are helping to preserve the family farm.

What is Community Supported Agriculture (CSA)?

The United States Department of Agriculture's Community Food Security Initiative is committed to creating and expanding 'grass-roots' partnerships that build local food systems and reduce hunger. If you are interested in *Community Supported Agriculture*, where consumers buy shares in local farms and receive food in return, you can call the Biodynamic Farming and Gardening Association in Pennsylvania who keep a national registry of 'CSA' farms and can refer you to one in your area.

For further information on this topic contact: www.sarep.ucdavis.edu. You can also look for farmers' market websites or contact your local Department of Agriculture office. For more general information on CSAs, you can write to: CSA West, c/o University of California, PO Box 363, Davis, CA 95617.

Gail Feenstra, M.Ed., Ed.D.
Food Systems Analyst, University of California, Davis

NUTRITIONAL PROFILE COMPARISON

Per serving	Nutrient Rich	Old Style
calories	404	600
fat (g)	8	28
saturated fat (g)	2	15
carbohydrates (g)	55	60
fiber (g)	8	8
sodium (mg)	545	1330

Seattle Summer Halibut
Seattle, Washington

When we host dinner parties, we set a place for a 'seventh guest' in recognition of people who are in need, homeless, or too ill to care for their own nutritional needs. Rather than serve the seventh guest, we make a donation to a social agency that helps the needy, like the remarkable 'FareStart' program in Seattle. Their 'good health' is part of our 'common wealth'.

I found this dish in Seattle, at the FareStart Restaurant on 2nd Avenue near the corner of Virginia, just a short walk over from the famous Pike Street Public Market. To be sure I had to reduce the oil used . . . however, the truly remarkable flavors still come out and get you! (P.S. You must like garlic for this one.)

Main Dishes

Ingredients:

Crostini
1 baguette
1/2 cup fish stock (see 'The Basics')
pinch saffron
1/8 teaspoon salt
1/8 teaspoon freshly ground pepper
extra virgin olive oil pan spray

Roasted Garlic Sauce
1 head garlic
1/2 cup yogurt cheese (see 'The Basics')
tiny pinch saffron
1 teaspoon extra virgin olive oil
1 tablespoon freshly squeezed lemon juice

Halibut
1 teaspoon extra virgin olive oil
6 cloves garlic, bashed and chopped
  (generous 2 tablespoons)
3 cups fish stock, divided
1 tablespoon chopped parsley
1/4 teaspoon salt
1 tablespoon freshly squeezed lemon juice
pinch saffron
4 6-ounce (170 g) halibut fillets
4 Roma tomatoes, cut in eighths lengthwise
  then in half crosswise
1 tablespoon arrowroot mixed with
  2 tablespoons fish stock or water (slurry)
3 tablespoons chopped parsley

Seattle Summer Halibut

1. Preheat the oven to 350°F (180°C). To make the crostini, cut the baguette in long diagonal slices starting the cuts from the top of the loaf. You will need 8 long thin slices. Heat the fish stock with the saffron, salt and pepper until it turns bright yellow. Brush the bread on both sides with the yellow broth. Spray lightly with the extra virgin olive oil pan spray. Bake on a baking sheet with a rack 5 minutes. Turn and bake 5 minutes more or until the bread is quite crisp. Set aside.

2. Cut the root end off the head of garlic and wrap in foil. Roast for an hour in the pre-heated oven or until very soft. Remove and cool before pressing out the cooked flesh. You should have 2 tablespoons. Combine with the yogurt cheese, saffron, olive oil, and lemon juice. Set aside.

3. Stir the olive oil and garlic together in a small saucepan on medium heat. Cook until it starts to sizzle, 2 minutes, then add 2 cups of the fish stock and parsley. Turn to high and reduce the liquid by half at a vigorous reducing boil, about 5 minutes. Strain into a skillet large enough to hold the fish fillets. Add the other cup of stock, salt, lemon juice, and saffron. Bring to a boil. Set the fillets in the stock and reduce the heat to medium. Cover with a sheet of waxed paper, cut to fit the pan. Simmer 5 minutes then turn and cook 2 minutes longer. Remove to 4 hot soup plates.

4. Toss the tomatoes into the boiling liquid to just heat through, 1 minute. Stir in the slurry and parsley. It should thicken almost immediately. Spoon over the fish fillets and serve with a dollop of the garlic sauce and 2 crostini. Scatter more chopped parsley over it if you like.

Serves 4

Special Techniques:

* Haybox Principle: place the halibut on a plate on a low heat burner covered by a metal trivet, and cover with a lid to finish off the cooking with steam heat. This will give you a tender piece of fish and will help to prevent over-cooking

Feeding the Homeless

FareStart is aptly named because it offers training to both men and women who, often through little fault of their own, become homeless. This non-profit organization has become world famous for its simple yet spectacular success with otherwise 'failed people'. Students are taught with donated foods that they prepare for homeless shelters and Head Start programs around the city. On Thursdays, the café is taken over by a guest chef who, with the student's help, prepares a wonderfully inventive dinner for the general public . . . it's a real sell out by the way. Cheryl Sesnon, the former Executive Director of this great organization, was my guest on The Gathering Place.

How does FareStart work?

We 'recruit' homeless people off the streets of Seattle. Most of these people became homeless when they were quite young and, up until the point of their participation in FareStart, had little hope for a better alternative. Individuals have to be ready to take a look at their life and make changes. The program offers weekly life skills training sessions that enhance social, mental, and physical skills. The recruits also need to want to cook, since they will be trained to prepare meals for others. Chef instructors as well as local guest chefs teach the FareStart participants to prepare the meals. The training program runs for 16 weeks and 90% of graduates are employed at graduation. There is a successful 70% retention rate at one year after graduation.

Cheryl Sesnon
Former Executive Director, FareStart Program

Who does FareStart feed?

FareStart serves over 2,000 meals a day through restaurants and catering services, including 350 people in homeless shelters, 900 children in daycare, and others in schools and Headstart programs.

How do you finance this operation?

About 60% of the full budget is earned through the various food service operations, while the remaining 40% of the budget comes from corporate donations, sponsors, and grants.

How can we make a difference in a person's life who is homeless?

NUTRITIONAL PROFILE COMPARISON

Per serving	Nutrient Rich	Old Style
calories	376	881
fat (g)	8	61
saturated fat (g)	1	9
carbohydrates (g)	32	40
fiber (g)	3	4
sodium (mg)	589	1078

You do not have to give them money to show respect or care. Simply smile. Look for a way to be respectful — a greeting, a short conversation, or a smile will often be the most appropriate action you can take.

For further information on this topic contact: www.farestart.org

St Augustine Perlow

St Augustine, Florida

How many calories do we need in a day? This depends on our weight and activity factor. To estimate a caloric framework for you, use this equation: multiply your weight in pounds _____ x your activity factor _____. For age 20-30, the activity factor is 13-15; for age 30-40, 12; for age 40-50, 11, for age 50 +, 10. Now do your homework! Remember, this is just an estimate — and never go below 1200 calories daily in your effort to lose weight. You need those calories to maintain good health.

This could be the mother of all spicy rice dishes of Southeastern and Southcentral USA! Clearly an import in the 1760s from the Southern Spanish coastline around Minorca, it is jambalaya-like in style and clearly a winner in the first settled city of the United States, St Augustine, Florida, where the local folks pronounced 'pilau' as 'per-low' — and so it has remained, a comforting southern classic. The datil pepper is one of those incendiary devices designed to 'blow your whistle' . . . hard! This raises the finished 'spice temperature' for the classic well above that of the jambalaya. The Minorcans brought the datil chile to the St Augustine area from Central or South America. St Augustine is the only place they grow now. These very hot chiles are a member of the capsicum sinense family that includes habanero and Scotch Bonnet chiles, the hottest in the world. These chiles can be mail ordered by calling Dat'l Do-It at 1-800-468-3285. Ask for a catalog of datil products. Tell Gina that Graham says, 'hi!

Main Dishes

Ingredients:

1 teaspoon non-aromatic olive oil
1 cup finely chopped onion
1 clove garlic, bashed and chopped
1/4-pound (115 g) Canadian bacon,
   cut in 1/2" (1.5 cm) dice
1 large red bell pepper,
   cut in 1/2" (1.5 cm) dice
4 Roma tomatoes, cut in 1/2" (1.5 cm) dice
3/4 cup celery, cut in 1/2" (1.5 cm) dice
1 teaspoon mild chili powder
1/4 teaspoon thyme
pinch cloves
1/4 teaspoon datil chile powder
   or cayenne pepper
2 bay leaves
1 teaspoon salt
1 cup washed long grain white rice
2 cups canned or homemade low sodium
   chicken stock (see 'The Basics')
1 cooked chicken breast, bone and skin
   removed, cut in large pieces
2 cooked chicken thighs, bone and skin
   removed, cut in large pieces
15 large black pitted olives, halved
2 tablespoons chopped parsley

St Augustine Perlow

1. Preheat the oven to 450°F (230°C). Heat the oil in a large skillet or chef's pan on medium-high. Sauté the onion 2 minutes or until it starts to wilt. Add the garlic and cook 1 minute more. Stir in the bacon, red pepper, tomatoes, celery, chili powder, thyme, cloves, datil or cayenne, bay leaves, and salt. Cook, stirring, 5 minutes more. Stir in the rice and pour the stock over all. Bake, uncovered, in the preheated oven 20 minutes or until the rice is tender and fluffy.

2. Poach the chicken by placing a piece of wax paper circle over the chicken that is cooking in water. When bubbles begin just under the wax paper, you know it is a good poaching temperature. It should take around 15 minutes to be cooked through, creating a nice moist piece of chicken.

3. Add the chicken and olives to the rice mixture, mix, and return to the oven for 6 more minutes to heat through. Serve on hot plates scattered with fresh parsley.

Serves 6

Home Food Safety

Did you know that 76 million people in the United States alone get sick every year from food-borne illness? Cooking is more than a question of flavor and nutrition — it's a question of safety! Registered Dietitian Joan Horbiak, who has performed the National Home Food Safety spokesperson duties for the American Dietetic Association, visited The Gathering Place to give us some tips on keeping your kitchen clean and safe.

Joan Horbiak, MPH, RD
Former National Home Food Safety Spokesperson, American Dietetic Association

How can we make food preparation safe?

Four simple steps can eliminate the majority of food borne illness:

1. Wash your hands often with warm water and soap for the length of time that it takes you to sing happy birthday for two choruses or 20 seconds. Nearly 50% of food-borne illness could be wiped out if we simply washed our hands this way.

2. Use separate chopping boards for raw meat/fish and poultry and another for your fruits and vegetables to eliminate cross-contamination of bacteria. It does not matter if the cutting board is wood, plastic, or ceramic. Remember, 'separate don't cross-contaminate'.

3. Cook foods properly by using a meat thermometer in the thickest part of the flesh. Chicken should be cooked to 160-170°F to be thoroughly and safely cooked. Consider that meat will continue cooking (up to 10 degrees) after pulling it out of the oven.

4. Refrigerate foods promptly. The refrigerator should be 40°F or lower and make sure you get foods into the refrigerator promptly after they are served.

Do you have any other 'safety' hints?

* High heat kills the bacteria, so use the dishwasher. You can also wash utensils and used cutting boards in hot soapy water and then rinse in a mixture of water and bleach: 1 quart of water and 2 teaspoons of bleach.

* Kitchen towels and sponges can easily carry bacteria, so wash them in a bleach bath and wash them often.

NUTRITIONAL PROFILE COMPARISON

Per serving	Nutrient Rich	Old Style
calories	275	446
fat (g)	7	20
saturated fat (g)	2	6
carbohydrates (g)	32	31
fiber (g)	2	3
sodium (mg)	661	1857

* Remove rings when you wash your hands, since bacteria can hide underneath the jewelry.

* Replace cutting boards if you have one with a crack or crevice since bacteria can accumulate here easily

For further information on this topic contact: www.homefoodsafety.org

Chiliquilies

Chicago, Illinois

Snacking has been given a bad reputation but it is actually a great habit if done wisely. One of the great 'guilty' pleasures of eating, snacking is a good way to get more nutrition in your diet. So snack away, without a guilty conscience. Just be sure to snack well!

Have you ever sat down to a great heaping plate of nachos, bathed in melting cheese and interspersed with olives and salsa? If so, then you know what WOW is in Mexican. So how about another WOW with half the fat of the old style traditional nachos dish? This is a truly superb dish served at Rick Bayless's wonderful Mexican restaurant in Chicago. If you just happen to be in that great city, do visit Frontera Grill or Topolobampo at 445 N Clark Street — and give Rick my very best regards.

Ingredients:

10 medium corn tortillas (12 oz)
1 can diced tomatoes,
  28-ounce (794 g), in juice
2 canned chipotle chilies, rinsed and seeded
  (if you like it blistering hot,
  leave the seeds)
1/2 teaspoon non-aromatic olive oil
1 large sweet onion, cut in 1/4" (.75 cm) dice,
  saving 1/2 cup for garnish
3 cloves garlic, bashed and chopped
2 cups canned or homemade low sodium
  chicken stock (see 'The Basics')
1/4 teaspoon salt

Garnish
1/2 cup low fat yogurt
1 1/2 cups shredded chicken
1/4 cup grated Parmesan cheese
1/2 cup chopped cilantro

Chiliquiles

1. Preheat the oven to 350° (180°C). Stack the tortillas and cut into eighths. Coat 2 baking sheets with pan spray and lay the tortilla wedges on them in one layer. Lightly spray the tops and bake 20 to 30 minutes or until crisp. Set aside.

2. Drain the tomatoes, reserving the liquid. Place the tomatoes in a blender jar with the chipotles and whiz until pureed but with some texture.

3. Heat the oil in a large, high-sided chef's pan or skillet on medium. Sauté the chopped onion until golden, about 7 minutes. Stir in the garlic and cook another minute. Raise the temperature to medium high and pour in the tomato puree. Cook, stirring often, until the sauce thickens and starts to spatter the stove, 5 minutes. Pour the reserved tomato juice into a measuring cup and add stock to make 2 1/2 cups. Add to the tomato mixture to make 4 1/2 cups of sauce altogether. Add salt and bring to a boil. Stir in the tortilla chips, making sure each one is coated with sauce. Bring back to the boil then remove from the heat. Cover and let set 5 minutes. No more!

4. Divide among 4 hot plates and top with the reserved onions, yogurt, chicken, cheese, and cilantro. The dish can also be served from the dish it was cooked in, topped attractively with the garnish.

Serves 4

Vegetarian Option: Chiliquiles

Use vegetable stock or water in place of the chicken stock. Slice and steam 2 chayote squash until tender as a substitute for the chicken.

Snacking Successfully

Snacking can be a habit that nourishes and sustains us — or a problematic source of excess calories and fat. Registered dietitian Kathleen Zelman came by The Gathering Place to show us how to select a variety of snack foods and make them part of a healthy diet. Wise snacks, with a careful eye on portion size, can provide great nutrition for children, teenagers, adults, and the elderly.

Should snacks be part of a healthy diet?

Yes, snacks can and should be an important part of an overall healthy diet, — even when we are trying to lose weight. But we need to choose, portion-controlled good snacks. Choose snacks with a 'mind for health'.

What is a good snack?

* Appropriate calories and portion size are key elements in determining a healthful snack.
* Snacks should encompass more than one food group with a balance of carbohydrate, a small amount of protein, and a small amount of fat.
* Snacks do not have to be the traditional 'snack' foods like pretzels, popcorn, or fruit: instead, they can be leftovers, fruit smoothies, and cereals too.
* Time your snacks so that you don't go over five hours without eating.
* Keep the calories within reason.

What foods do you suggest for snacks?

* Grains: pack cereal, crackers, and rice cakes in a single-serve container for snacking on the run.
* Fruits and Vegetables: pack fresh cut vegetables in zipper lock storage bags.
* Milk / Yogurt / Cheese: look for individually wrapped cheese sticks and slices or single-serve yogurt containers.
* Meat / Fish / Poultry / Dry Beans / Eggs / Nuts: 1/2 tuna fish or turkey breast sandwich can make a satisfying and great snack.

Kathleen Zelman, MPH, RD
Nutrition Consultant
Spokesperson, American Dietetic Association

NUTRITIONAL PROFILE COMPARISON

Per serving	Nutrient Rich	Vegetarian	Old Style
calories	386	301	482
fat (g)	8	5	17
saturated fat (g)	3	2	6
carbohydrates (g)	50	53	55
fiber (g)	7	7	8
sodium (mg)	820	777	981

What are the largest snacking pitfalls?

* Large, jumbo, and super-size portions result in excess calories and fat — for example, a super-size muffin at 400 calories and 30 grams of fat. Cut the muffin in half or even quarters — or select a smaller size.

* Eating 'out of the bag' because you don't know how much you are eating without portioning out your snack. Measure out a portion and put the bag away.

* Excessive soft drinks for kids. Consider fruit juices instead, which can provide nutrition when chosen wisely. Avoid juices that contain high fructose corn syrup and sugar from sources other than the natural fruit.

Do you have any additional snacking suggestions?

1. Curb Mindless Munching: Often we snack out of habit or without our wits about us. Maintain a level of consciousness so that you know what you are eating.
2. Substitute or Limit Portions: At meetings and social functions when you are offered muffins, pastries,and cookies, decline, opt for a bagel, fresh fruit, low-calorie beverages or take half of one of the foods offered.

For additional information and a copy of Snacking Habits for Healthy Living contact: 1-800-366-1655 or www.eatright.org.

Roast Chicken

New York, New York

More 'numbers'! It is not just what we weigh but where the fat is located on the body that defines our health risk. Aim for a waist/hip ratio of .95 for men and .85 for women; and a waist measurement of less than 40 inches or one meter for men, 36 inches or 90 cm for women. Research indicates that anything above these numbers increases our health risk.

Roast chicken must now be the most familiar food on North America's comfort scale . . . perhaps with well-buttered creamed potatoes on the side? The thought of crisp, well seasoned, fatty skin is . . . well . . . lustful? So, if the skin is to go (and drop almost 200 calories per serving), what can be done to reserve taste, aroma, color, and texture? Well, this family-style dish with vegetables shows you how! A delicious, attractive way to serve a naked bird. If, by chance, you don't care for ginger, then use green onions or thin slices of garlic in lieu. Also, be sure you have a 'mild' paprika; some 'say' they are mild but wind up with quite a kick. Personally I like the extra 'touch', but it may meet some resistance from the youngsters!

Main Dishes

Ingredients:

Vegetables

2 tablespoons freshly squeezed lemon juice
1/2 teaspoon ground ginger
1/2 teaspoon salt
1/2 teaspoon paprika
1/4 teaspoon freshly ground black pepper
1 teaspoon fresh or dried rosemary, chopped
4 medium carrots, peeled and cut in half
  lengthwise and again across
4 small parsnips, peeled and
  cut like the carrots
3/4-pound Yellow Finn or Yukon Gold
  potatoes, quartered

Chicken

1 whole 3-pound (1,350 g) chicken
1 good size knob fresh ginger root, thinly
  sliced, peel on
1/2 lemon, thinly sliced
2 tablespoons freshly squeezed lemon juice
1/4 teaspoon paprika, divided
1 teaspoon arrowroot mixed with
  2 teaspoons water (slurry)
1 tablespoon chopped parsley

Roast Chicken

1. Preheat the oven to 350°F (180°C). Combine the lemon juice, ginger, salt, paprika, pepper and rosemary and toss together in a large bowl with the cut vegetables. Tip out into a baking pan and spray lightly with olive oil pan spray and roast 25 minutes.

2. Cut the chicken along both sides of the breastbone. Separate and discard the bone. Now cut through the ribs along the backbone and save for stocks later on. You will now have two separate halves of chicken ready to roast. Cut through the skin around the thigh and slide 3 thin slices of ginger under the skin of the breast, thigh and leg of each half. Turn over and place 3 more slices of ginger, then 3 slices of lemon in the cavity on the bony side. Set each chicken half, skin side up on a piece of foil and pinch the foil up around the edges leaving the skin exposed. This will hold the seasonings close to the meat and catch the flavorful juice. Place on a rack in a baking pan and start roasting after the vegetables have cooked 25 minutes. Roast 35 minutes, leaving the vegetables in for a total of 1 hour.

3. Remove the vegetables from the oven and keep warm. Pour the juice accumulated in the foil into a fat strainer. Discard the skin, ginger, and lemon slices from the chicken halves, leaving the skin on the wings. Bone the breasts and lay them with the wings in a skillet large enough for all the pieces. Separate the legs from the thighs. Lay in the skillet with the breasts. Cut the ends off the legs, leaving the bone in and arrange in the pan with the rest of the chicken. Pour in the de-fatted juice. Coat with lemon juice, sprinkle evenly with 1/8 teaspoon of the paprika and set under the broiler 5 minutes or until golden brown.

4. Arrange the chicken and vegetables on a large hot platter. Bring the juice in the pan to a boil, add the remaining 1/8 teaspoon paprika and thicken with the slurry. Stir in the parsley. Pour over the chicken and vegetables and serve to a hungry family.

Serves 4

Reliable Health Research

Every day new health and nutrition information comes 'hot off the press', but we need to be leery of claims that sound too good to be true, Professor Rena Mendelson advises us. Worthwhile research will stand the test of time. We need good clinical trials to prove any claim. Save yourself possible frustration and disappointment, even health risk, the next time you hear about the 'quick fix' or 'magic bullet'. Always consult your family physician about questions you have regarding your health.

What happens when people rush out to buy a 'great' new pill, diet, or health fix?

They often take too much because they think more is better and unwittingly become their own experimental guinea pigs. This 'experiment' will often tell us something the manufacturers never claimed or suspected about side effects. For example, we recently learned that taking excessive vitamin B6 to treat carpal tunnel syndrome may actually cause nerve damage.

Rena A. Mendelson, D.Sc., MS
Associate Vice-President Academic, Ryerson
Polytechnic University

How do we sort out the valid from the invalid claims?

Start by asking a few basic questions:
* Does it sound too good to be true?
* Who did the research? Consider the source of the information.
* Was the research trying to answer a scientific question or develop a commercial product?
* Am I asked to do something way outside of the recommended levels? Be leery, if this is the case.

So, the next time you read or hear about a scientific claim, consider this:

* Think very carefully about doing anything that is way out of the norm for treating ourselves. Keep within a framework that works for you.
* Remember that not one research study will give us the whole story, but rather an accumulation of knowledge over time.
* Use health professionals (physician along with a registered dietitian) as a filter between scientific evidence and practice, and when you have any health-related questions.

NUTRITIONAL PROFILE COMPARISON

Per serving	Nutrient Rich	Old Style
calories	494	686
fat (g)	11	28
saturated fat (g)	3	8
carbohydrates (g)	50	53
fiber (g)	7	6
sodium (mg)	473	804

What else can we do?

There are some basic tools for steering us in the right direction with regard to research and diet. The Canada Food Guide and the US Food Guide Pyramid as well as many other international dietary establishments have been developed as a result of a wealth of research. The information available from these organizations are recommendations that give us a foundation to make sound and appropriate health choices. Something that steers significantly from these recommendations should be suspect.

Boston Baked Beans

Boston, Massachusetts

Eating can and should be a pleasurable experience. When you learn to focus on consuming the abundance of natural and healthy foods available instead of limiting yourself to a special 'diet', you will not only be on your way to wellness, but you will find joy in eating as well.

Just for fun — walk up the aisles of your favorite supermarket and just see how much space is allocated to canned beans; it's really amazing how widespread their appeal is (and how much pig fat is added to some!) This method bows to the classic, but removes the 8 ounces of salt pork, choosing instead half the quantity of good lean Canadian bacon. This drops the fat by 13 grams, which in turn, lowers calories by just over 200 per portion from the Old Style. The flavor is excellent and the texture is classic, even though it doesn't look like canned beans. After all, remember what canning does to spaghetti!

Ingredients:

1 pound navy beans, soaked overnight
1/2 teaspoon baking soda
1 medium onion, peeled
1/4 cup brown sugar
1/4 cup molasses
1 teaspoon dry mustard
1 1/2 teaspoons salt
1/4 teaspoon black pepper
1/2 teaspoon non-aromatic olive oil
1/4-pound (113 g) Canadian bacon
    cut in 1/2 inch (1.25 cm) chunks
boiling water to cover

Boston Baked Beans

1. Bring a large pot of water to a boil. Drain the soaked beans and add to the boiling water with the soda. Boil 15 minutes. Place the onion in the bottom of a bean pot or other baking dish with a small opening. You can also put a collar of foil over a small bowl and wrap it tightly, leaving a 2-inch diameter hole in the middle. Drain the beans and return to the pan.

2. Preheat the oven to 300°F (150°C). Combine the brown sugar, molasses, mustard, salt, and pepper in a small bowl. Heat the oil in a small skillet on medium high. Sauté the bacon 2 minutes to release the flavors. Add a teaspoon of the molasses mixture and stir while cooking 1 more minute. Stir into the drained beans with the rest of the molasses mixture and pour over the onion in the bean pot. De-glaze the pan with a little water and pour over the beans.

3. Cover with boiling water and bake in the preheated oven 6 hours or until the beans are tender and the sauce, syrupy. Stir every once in a while but don't add water unless it gets really dry. Serve with Boston Brown Bread.

Serves 6

Vegetarian Option:

You can leave out the Canadian bacon if you prefer to cook this dish with no meat.

Special Techniques:

* To decrease the 'gas' in beans, add 1 teaspoon of baking soda to the beans that are cooking.

Exploring Folic Acid

We invited Registered Dietitian Evelyn Tribole back to The Gathering Place to discuss a special nutrient, folate (folic acid), a 'B' vitamin, which has been shown not only to prevent birth defects but also to lower heart attack risk. While we can 'supplement' this vitamin into our diet, we can also simply eat more beans!

What is folic acid?

Folate is an 'essential' B vitamin involved in every single cell in our body. While this nutrient is found in many foods, the man-made version of folate is called folic acid.

What is the importance of folate for our health?

* Folate is important for the prevention of heart disease by controlling our homocysteine levels. High levels are often associated with people who do not get enough folate in their diet. The test for homocysteine is not a routine test at this point, so you may want to ask your physician to check this value if you are concerned.

* Folate is important for women who are of child-bearing age and planning to start a family. Research shows that if women were to get 400 micrograms of folate a day, we could prevent over 50% of neural-tube birth defects.

Evelyn Tribole, MS, RD
Nutrition Consultant and Author, *Stealth Health*

How much folate do we need in our daily diet?

The recommendation is for individuals, both men and women, to consume 400 micrograms of folate a day.

What are common dietary sources of folate?

1. Beans are the best source (1 cup of beans equals 200 micrograms of folate)
2. Broccoli
3. Strawberries
4. Asparagus
5. Most dark leafy greens
6. Orange juice

NUTRITIONAL PROFILE COMPARISON

Per serving	Nutrient Rich	Vegetarian	Old Style
calories	270	254	418
fat (g)	2	1	15
saturated fat (g)	1	.23	5
carbohydrates (g)	50	50	50
fiber (g)	14	14	14
sodium (mg)	642	451	905

In the United States, it is law that foods with flour are to be enriched with folic acid.

For further information on this topic contact: www.eatright.org and read Evelyn's book, *Stealth Health*

$\mathcal{J}$ambalaya
New Orleans, Louisiana

$\mathcal{M}$ore math! BMI (Body Mass Index) = weight in kilograms/(height in meters) ^{2}. BMI is one more measure that will help us to better understand our health. For me at 90 kilograms and 2 meters, my BMI is 90 kg/2x2 or 90/4 = 23. The World Health Organization rates a BMI of 20-25 as normal, 25-30 overweight, and above 30, obese. Sometimes just doing the math reduces weight!

This dish arrived with the Spanish in the late 1700s when their influence was strongly felt in New Orleans. Since ham was the only main ingredient used, it took the name 'jamon', Spanish for ham. This is similar to the French 'jambon' that came later and fit equally well. Then the idea of F.A.B.I.S. (fresh and best in season) took over to make up the great Creole regional dish we now call Jambalaya. My version of the classic simply uses oil as needed, and I've used the excellent, new, lower fat, yet spicy sausages available today. Lean Canadian-styled bacon provides the essential jamon flavor. We all love this dish — it's one of our favorite comfort foods.

Ingredients:

2 cups low sodium chicken broth
1/2 pound (225 g) medium shrimp,
  peeled and de-veined
1 cup long grain white rice
1/8 teaspoon salt
3 bay leaves
1 1/2 teaspoons non-aromatic olive oil,
  divided
3 spicy low fat chicken sausages (12 oz, 340 g)
1 large sweet onion, cut in half
  and sliced stem to root
4 cloves garlic, bashed and chopped
1 tablespoon tomato paste
1 large rib celery cut in 1 1/2" (4 cm) strips
1 large red bell pepper cut in 1 1/2"
  (4 cm) strips
3 ounces (85 g) Canadian bacon,
  cut in 1 1/2" (4 cm) strips
1/4 teaspoon cayenne pepper
1/4 teaspoon thyme
pinch ground cloves
8 Roma tomatoes, peeled, seeded,
  and chopped or 1 can, 28 ounce (794 g),
  diced tomatoes in juice
1/4 cup chopped parsley

Jambalaya

1. Bring the stock to a boil in a medium saucepan. Drop the shrimp in and cook 3 minutes. Remove shrimp and set aside. Measure the stock and add water to make 2 cups. Add the rice, salt, and bay leaves and cook 15 minutes or until tender and the liquid gone. Set aside.

2. Heat 1 teaspoon of the oil in a 10 1/2" (26.5 cm) chef's pan and fry the sausages, turning often, 11 minutes on medium-high or until nearly done. Cut in rounds and set aside.

3. Pour the remaining 1/2 teaspoon oil into the pan and sauté the onion until it turns translucent, 3 to 4 minutes. Add the garlic and tomato paste and continue cooking until the paste darkens. Now toss in the celery, red pepper and Canadian bacon and cook until the vegetables are crisp tender. Season with cayenne, thyme and cloves. Stir in the tomatoes, parsley, reserved shrimp and sausage, and cook until just heated through. Add the rice and mix well.

Serves 6

African American Health Issues

I strongly believe that the African American table is a wonderful example for us all to follow. It's because of attitude, not necessarily nutrition, though. So much of life's pure joys are played out at a comforting gathering where good food says, 'See how much I love you'. This is the attitude we need to bring to our table . . . yet at the same time we can exercise loving restraint in the use of fat and refined carbohydrates, as registered dietitian Jeannette Jordan advised us when she appeared on The Gathering Place.

What are the most prevalent health concerns in the African American population?

* Diabetes
* Obesity
* High blood pressure

Most of these problems can all be related to and affected by the diet.

What are the key dietary recommendations for this population?

1. Decreasing Total Fat: The importance of decreasing total fat intake is paramount. Fried and fatty foods are so prevalent that sometimes these foods are consumed two to three times a day.

2. Monitoring Calories: Large glasses of sweet tea and colas seem to be an issue since they are laden with calories.

3. Increasing Fiber: There is a need to increase high fiber fruits, vegetables, and whole grains.

4. Understanding Portion Size: Proper portion size is often misunderstood.

How can traditional foods African-American foods be prepared with less fat?

* Eliminate bacon, 'fatback', or fatty meat by using different flavorings or substitute with lean turkey or ham.
* Fat should always be trimmed off meats whenever possible.
* Alternative ways of seasoning foods should be tested.

Jeannette Jordan, MS, RD, CDE
Prevention/Detection Education Coordinator,
Medical University of South Carolina
Author, *Good Health Cookbook*
Spokesperson, American Dietetic Association

NUTRITIONAL PROFILE COMPARISON

Per serving	Nutrient Rich	Old Style
calories	270	482
fat (g)	4	20
saturated fat (g)	1	7
carbohydrates (g)	39	48
fiber (g)	3	2
sodium (mg)	573	1561

What else can be done to improve the health of African Americans?

Exercise is a key recommendation in addition to making dietary changes because it helps to lower blood pressure. Exercise also helps control diabetes and improves weight loss and weight maintenance. Research shows that regular intermittent exercise throughout the day can be extremely beneficial for one's health (you don't have to do it all at once to get the benefit).

For further information on this topic contact: www.eatright.org and read Jeannette Jordan's *Good Health Cookbook*. For this cookbook, telephone 843-876-1949

hrimp Gumbo
New Orleans, Louisiana

'Good for you' and 'good tasting' — these are two phrases we seldom associate. Somehow we came to believe that nutritious food was not delicious and vice versa. By stopping to learn the language of food, negative mindsets can be reversed and the joy of eating can begin. By focusing on creative techniques and buying the freshest food to begin with, the art of serving great food for optimal health can be mastered — and savored!

Many years ago I visited a great restaurant in New Orleans that was reported to serve the finest shrimp gumbo in town. The restaurant is called 'Dooky Chase' and the chef/owner is Leah Chase. Not only was it good then, it's still great today and well worth a visit. I've made adjustments over the years as my understanding of what it means to be moderate has changed, but to my senses it still looks, tastes, and smells simply wonderful.

Main Dishes

Shrimp Gumbo

Ingredients:

1-pound (450 g) medium shrimp
1 cup uncooked long grain white rice
3 teaspoons non-aromatic olive oil, divided
1/4-pound (113 g) Canadian bacon, cut in
  1/2" (1.5 cm) dice (scant 3/4 cup)
1 1/2 cups chopped onion
2 cloves garlic, bashed and chopped
1 cup celery, cut in 1/2" (1.5 cm) slices
1 large red bell pepper, cut in 1/4" (.75 cm)
  dice (generous cup)
3 tablespoons tomato paste
2 cups frozen or fresh sliced okra
  (1/2" or .75 cm slices)
1/4 cup all purpose flour
2 cups shrimp shell stock
1/4 teaspoon cayenne pepper
1/2 teaspoon dried thyme
2 bay leaves
1 teaspoon gumbo filé (optional)
2 tablespoons chopped parsley (optional)

1. Shell and de-vein the shrimp, reserving the shells. Pour 4 cups water over the shells in a large saucepan and bring to a boil. Reduce the heat and simmer 2 minutes. Strain and reserve. Use 2 cups of the liquid to cook the rice. Bring to a boil, add rice, then cover and reduce to a simmer for about 15 minutes until all moisture is absorbed. Save the rest of the liquid for the gumbo.

2. Heat 1 teaspoon of the oil in a skillet or chef's pan on medium high. Sauté the Canadian bacon 2 minutes. Add the onions and cook until they start to wilt, 2 minutes. Add the garlic, celery, and red pepper and continue to sauté 3 to 4 minutes. Pull the vegetables to the side of the pan and add the tomato paste. Cook, stirring, until it darkens, then stir in the vegetables. Remove to a plate.

3. Heat the remaining oil in the same pan. Shake the okra in the flour in a bag. Pour into a strainer to remove extra flour. Brown the floured okra in the hot oil. Return the vegetables to the pan and add the remaining shrimp liquid. Season with the cayenne, thyme and bay and simmer until the okra is tender, about 10 minutes. Stir in the shrimp and cook until pink. Add the filé and simmer 5 minutes until thickened. Please DON'T boil after adding filé. The gumbo will be pretty thick so this step isn't absolutely necessary.

4. Divide the rice among 4 hot soup plates and pour the Gumbo over the top. Garnish with chopped fresh parsley if you like.

Serves 4

Gourmet-Style Hospital Food Service

Gourmet-style hospital food service? Surely, you must be joking. Nutritious, yes, but delicious, no . . . Doesn't it have to 'hurt' to be good for you? But in many hospitals today the art of cooking and the science of nutrition have mingled to create delicious and satisfying hospital food service — as our guest, Mary Kimbrough, a registered dietitian at Zale Lipshy University Hospital in Dallas, Texas explained on The Gathering Place. Healing has a lot to do with not only the nutritional value but also the comfort of good tasting food. You can eat healthier by following these recommendations in your home, too!

What are current trends in hospital food service?

The hospital should be a model for health and wellness. But if you speak the 'language' of diets, restricting meals by cutting out salt, sugar, and fat without regard for flavor, the food will be boring and bland and will not motivate the people that truly need to make a change. We need flavor to encourage change.

How do you achieve 'good-tasting' food that is 'good for you'?

We've made a commitment to achieving this combination of 'good-tasting' and 'good-for-you' food from the top down, from management to food service worker. Dietitians have partnered with chefs to make it successful so that taste and health can go hand in hand. We've also discovered that by establishing the fundamentals of developing full flavor foods you can reduce the number of diets to just two: regular and special requests.

What techniques are used to make food delicious and nutritious?

* Fresh veggies are served in salads with and fat-free dressings.
* The freshest seasonal fruit is served daily.
* Lean meats are prepared healthfully, without sacrificing flavor.
* Meats are served with salsas, slaws, and purees.
* Meat is served in a 3-4 oz. portion and paired with vegetables and starches.
* Healthy oils are used.

Mary Kimbrough, RD, LD
Director, Nutrition Services,
Zale Lipshy University Hospital

NUTRITIONAL PROFILE COMPARISON

Per serving	Nutrient Rich	Old Style
calories	414	588
fat (g)	7	20
saturated fat (g)	2	2
carbohydrates (g)	53	55
fiber (g)	5	4
sodium (mg)	637	1509

* Vegetables are enhanced with herbs, stocks, and aromatics.
* Low fat dairy products are used.
* Menus feature plant-based entrees.
* Variety is stressed.

For more information, contact: Zale Lipshy University Hospital Foodservice at www.zluh.org

Chicken à la King
New York, New York

Are you 'diet ready'? Often we know that something is right for us but we don't do it. The challenge is to find a time when you are ready to make a dietary change so that change can take place successfully. Sometimes, unfortunately, it takes a health problem to make us change our lifestyle. Why not change your diet and lifestyle now to improve your health before change becomes necessary?

Oh my . . . there are so many likely stories to be told about how this chicken got its name (such as the reason for crossing the road!). Most likely, Chef George Greenwald of the Brighton Beach Hotel in New York copied it from London's Claridge's Hotel or even from Delmonico's 'a la Keene', named for one of their regulars. I'm going for the London original because it used an egg and cream liaison much in vogue at the time. Of course, that same ultra-rich and overpowering sauce has now gone right out of fashion, and so I'd love it if you would just try my velvet smooth yogurt sauce, just to see if it still makes the grade? To be sure, there is a 200 calorie difference and 37 fewer fat grams. However, in its place there are wonderfully vivid fresh flavors to enjoy . . . especially the tarragon. This is so good that a scattering of fresh tarragon on the top at service would be just dandy!

Main Dishes

Ingredients:

1 whole frying chicken, about 3 1/2 pounds
8 cups water or to cover chicken
Bouquet Garni (see 'The Basics')

Rice
3 cups chicken broth
  (from cooked chicken above)
1/2 cup wild rice
1/4 teaspoon salt
1/2 cup long grain white rice

Sauce
3 cups chicken broth
  (from cooked chicken above)
1 large red bell pepper, chopped 1" dice
12 medium mushrooms, quartered
1/8 teaspoon ground nutmeg
1/4 teaspoon salt
1/4 teaspoon pepper
1/8 teaspoon cayenne (optional)
3 tablespoons cornstarch mixed with
  6 tablespoons water (slurry)
1 cup nonfat yogurt cheese (see 'The Basics')

Garnish
chopped parsley
chopped fresh tarragon (optional)

Chicken à la King

1. Rinse the chicken, place in a large pan, and cover with water. Place the bouquet garni ingredients in an herb ball or tie up in cheesecloth and add. Bring to a boil, reduce the heat and simmer 1 hour or until chicken is tender. Skim off the scum as it rises to the surface. Remove the chicken to a plate and strain the broth into a fat strainer. Pour 3 cups of the de-fatted broth into a saucepan and 3 cups into a 10 1/2" (26.5 cm) chef's pan. Save the rest (if there is any) for another purpose. When the chicken is cool enough, remove and discard the skin and bones. Pull the meat apart into bite size pieces and set aside.

2. Bring the broth in the saucepan to a boil and add the wild rice and salt. Cover and boil gently for 30 minutes. Add the white rice and continue cooking another 15 minutes or until tender. Take off the heat and set aside.

3. Bring the broth in the chef's pan to a hearty boil and reduce to 2 cups, 10 minutes. Add the peppers, mushrooms, nutmeg, salt, pepper, and optional cayenne and simmer 2 minutes. Add the chicken. Stir in the slurry and boil 30 seconds to cook the cornstarch. Place the yogurt cheese in a 4 cup measuring cup or bowl. Stir 1 cup of the thickened sauce into the yogurt to temper. Pour into the chicken mixture and mix well.

4. Serve with a 3/4 cup mound of the rice and steamed snow peas or sugar snaps.

Serves 6

Special Techniques:

* When boiling a whole chicken always put the breast down for better cooking.

* 'Tempering' requires pouring a small portion of hot liquid into a cold substance like yogurt and mixing; you can then add the mixed liquid back into the warmer dish and it will not break. This 'tempering' technique works well when you are dealing with milk products.

Managing Stress

Psychologist Jeff Janata returned to The Gathering Place to see how I was coping with the stress of preparing Chicken à la King and to share more helpful information about stress in our lives. This information seems so valuable that it bears discussing often. Because stress is inevitable in our lives, we always need to keep working at ways to reduce it. Let's see what else Jeff has to say . . .

What are the key tools and strategies people can use in order to manage stress?

Remember we are not trying to eliminate stress, but just get it to a middle range. To do so, try the following:

* Keep a 'stress diary' of things that instigate the felling of stress to create a self-awareness.

* Problem solve — try to work through areas that appear to be most stressful.

* Exercise to reduce stress — which is also good for your health.

* Take a break away from any stressful environment, even if it is just a quick trip to the drinking fountain. Studies of business executives who take a very brief break showed reduced stress levels and reduced absenteeism.

* Seek medical help. Medicine may become necessary when other strategies are not enough. Realize you are not a failure when medicine is part of the treatment, but instead recognize the success of being able to control your health.

Here, then, are 'three steps to less stress':

1. Be aware of stress and how stress affects your health. Don't deny feeling stress at work or at home. Try to identify the causes.

2. Figure out which causes are within your control and plan strategies to solve these problems and minimize stress.

3. Develop ways to manage stressful situations that are not necessarily within your control. Anticipate these situations and make these problems transparent so you can see successful ways of handling them with the minimum of stress.

For further information on this topic contact: http://www.apa.org/psychnet/

Jeff Janata, PhD
Psychologist, University Hospitals of Cleveland

NUTRITIONAL PROFILE COMPARISON

Per serving	Nutrient Rich	Old Style
calories	336	547
fat (g)	6	43
saturated fat (g)	2	6
carbohydrates (g)	34	43
fiber (g)	2	2
sodium (mg)	387	1073

Cabbage Rolls
Chicago, Illinois

Gaining weight is like putting handfuls of pleasure-soaked feathers on a balance scale. Losing weight is removing them one at a time. It takes patience and consistency to eat a little less and move a little more every day, but it's the best way to make this vital change in your 'health' behavior.

This is another great example of comfort food. It is typically Northern European Slavic and often found in communities where the sweet-sour 'clash' of tastes could somehow roll back the leaden clouds of winter. I'm very fond of this recipe, so much so that I find it hard to keep to the two rolls per serving!

Main Dishes

Ingredients:

1 large head green cabbage
  (9-10 inches in diameter)
1 teaspoon non-aromatic olive oil
2 cups finely chopped sweet onions
4 cloves garlic, bashed and chopped
6-ounces leanest ground beef (9%)
6-ounces ground white meat turkey
1/4 cup raw long grain white rice
2 tablespoons tomato puree
1/4 cup beef broth
1/4 teaspoon dried dill weed
1/4 teaspoon salt
1/4 teaspoon freshly ground black pepper
2 tablespoons chopped parsley

Sauce

1 1/2 cups tomato puree
1 1/2 cups beef broth
1/4 cups packed brown sugar
1/2 cup cider vinegar
1/4 teaspoon freshly ground black pepper
1/4 teaspoon dried dill weed
1/4 teaspoon caraway seed
3 bay leaves
2 teaspoons arrowroot mixed with
  2 tablespoons water (slurry)

Cabbage Rolls

1. Preheat the oven to 350°F (180°C.) Spray a 9" x 13" (23 x 33 cm) baking pan. Fill a large pan with water, cover and bring to a boil. Carve the core out of the cabbage and place in the boiling water to cook, covered, for 10 minutes. Take out of the boiling water and plunge into a bowl of cold water to cool.

2. Heat the oil in a chef's pan on medium high. Drop the onions into the hot pan and cook 3 minutes or until they begin to turn translucent. Add the garlic and cook 1 more minute. Place half the onion garlic mixture in a large bowl. Leave the rest in the pan to make the sauce. Combine the ground beef and turkey, rice, tomato puree, broth, dill weed, salt, pepper, and parsley with the onion mixture in the bowl.

3. Pour the tomato puree, broth, brown sugar, vinegar, pepper, dill weed, caraway, and bay leaves into the pan with the reserved onion and garlic and simmer while you make the rolls, about 15 minutes.

4. Drain the cabbage and separate 12 of the largest cabbage leaves without tearing. Cut out the center heavy rib from each leaf leaving a shallow 'V' shape. Spread out on the kitchen bench. Divide the filling among the leaves (a heaping tablespoon is about right). Overlap the sides where you removed the stems, fold over the sides first and then roll to completely enclose the filling.

5. Set them side by side in the prepared pan and pour the sauce over all, lay a piece of foil on top. Bake in the preheated oven, covered, for 1 hour. Remove the foil and bake 1/2 hour longer.

6. Divide the cabbage rolls among 6 warm plates. Pour the sauce into a saucepan and thicken with the arrowroot slurry. Spoon over the waiting rolls.

Serves 6

Classically a broad buttered noodle would be served, but I prefer a mashed potato spiked with horseradish and a broiled beef-steak tomato half.

Changing Your Diet for Good

From Dr James Prochaska, author of Changing for Good, we learn that behavior change is an individual process. Each person should be able to identify a stage of change where they currently stand. With appropriate awareness and tailored direction, people can move through the 'stages of change' in order to accomplish their health behavior goals. I urge you to check in to this one so that you can make changes that are beneficial and life lasting!

How can we minimize resistance to change and maximize participation in positive health behavior?

We need to look at change as something that occurs in five stages:
1. Precontemplation: We're not ready to change and may have given up on our ability to change .
2. Contemplation: We are thinking about change, but still have real doubts.
3. Preparation: We are taking small steps to change and have considered a plan for change.
4. Action: We have made overt change for less than six months.
5. Maintenance: We have made overt change for more than six months and are prepared for times of distress so we don't return to old habits.

James Prochaska, PhD
Director, Cancer Prevention Research Center, and Professor of Psychology, University of Rhode Island
Author, Changing for Good

Making a change transparent is on the average a 7-10 year process if you are working on your own, and about 12 months with the correct guidance.

How do we make the big move from 'precontemplation' to 'contemplation'?

People in the precontemplative stage generally experience a lack of information. They are not aware of the many benefits of making change — healthier heart, healthier brain, better sleep, and more. The key is to become educated. Find a qualified health professional who can guide you and monitor your progress.

How do we prevent a 'relapse' into unhealthy behavior?

Historically, relapse was considered a failure, but we need to see it as a learning experience.

NUTRITIONAL PROFILE COMPARISON

Per serving	Nutrient Rich	Old Style
calories	249	404
fat (g)	7	22
saturated fat (g)	2	9
carbohydrates (g)	32	24
fiber (g)	6	4
sodium (mg)	291	1183

Ask yourself, what did I do wrong? What mistake did I make? What am I going to do differently next time I make a mistake. The only true mistake is to give up on your ability to change.

For further information on this topic contact: www.prochange.com and read Dr Prochaska's book, *Changing for Good*

Nora's Shrimp and Mushroom Risotto

Washington, DC

*F*iber in our diet helps to fight the 'Big (Bad) Five' — heart disease, diabetes, high blood pressure, cancer, and obesity. While the recommended level of fiber in our diet is 25-30 grams per day, the average American consumes only half this much. A sure way to solve this problem is to eat more whole fruits, vegetables, and grains — ideally, organically grown!

Let me first tell you a little about Nora. This is her basic idea — a succulent risotto that isn't loaded down with oil, butter, and cheese but filled with glorious, fresh, organic flavors. Nora is the first person I know to operate a restaurant entirely on organic principles. The food is truly wonderful and alive with great flavors, and boy does the menu honor the farmers from whom she obtains such excellent produce. For anyone who truly wants to test whether organic really does make a difference, then a trip to Nora's in Washington, DC is an essential and always a rewarding experience. My version uses dried wild mushrooms combined with fresh ones, since at the time I was cooking, the fresh ones were buried in snow!

Main Dishes

Ingredients:

Rice

1 teaspoon non-aromatic olive oil
1/4 cup minced shallots
5 large cloves garlic, bashed and chopped
1 1/2 cups arborio rice
   (plump rice grain used in risotto dishes)
2 cups de-alcoholized dry white wine
3 cups low sodium chicken stock
1/4 teaspoon saffron threads

Garnish

4 teaspoons non-aromatic olive oil, divided
3 cloves garlic, bashed and chopped
1/2-pound (225-g) cremini mushrooms,
   wiped and sliced in 3 pieces
1 teaspoon wild mushroom powder
   (optional)
2 tablespoons freshly squeezed lemon juice,
   divided
1/2 teaspoon salt
1/4 teaspoon freshly ground pepper
1-pound (450-g) medium shrimp,
   shelled and de-veined
1 cup low sodium stock
1 cup de-alcoholized dry white wine
1/2 bunch spinach, stemmed
   and cut in thin strips
1 cup frozen petit peas
2 tablespoons chopped chives
   or parsley for garnish
6 tablespoons fresh grated parmesan cheese,
   optional (*not* included in the nutritional
   numbers — adds 2 grams of fat per serving)

Nora's Shrimp and Mushroom Risotto

1. Heat the oil in a skillet or chef's pan on medium high. Sauté the shallots until tender and transparent, 3 minutes. Add the garlic and cook 1 minute more. Stir in the rice and fry until it starts to look translucent, 2 minutes. Combine the wine and stock in a saucepan and heat. Add 1 cup of the liquid to the rice, bring to a boil, reduce the heat, add the saffron and simmer until the liquid is absorbed. Keep adding liquid 1 cup at a time, stirring frequently, until the rice is al dente, about 20 minutes. You may not need all the liquid to achieve al dente rice. If you have some left, use it at the end to reheat the risotto. Spread the rice on a baking sheet to cool.

2. Heat 3 teaspoons of the oil in the pan on medium high. Add the garlic to break out the flavors, 30 seconds, and toss in the mushrooms. Sprinkle with the mushroom powder and sauté until tender, 2 minutes. Season with the lemon juice, salt and pepper. Tip out onto a plate.

3. Heat the remaining oil. Sauté the shrimp 2 minutes or until pink. Pour in the stock and wine. Return the mushrooms, and risotto to the pan to heat through. Stir in the spinach and peas and cook 2 minutes or until bright green. Sprinkle with the remaining lemon juice. Divide among 6 hot soup plates. Garnish with chives or parsley.

Serves 6

Special Technique:

To make your own wild mushroom powder, start with a small package of dried wild mushrooms. Grind to a powder in a clean coffee grinder. Store in a jar and use when needed for extra mushroom flavor.

Organic Food

Nora's restaurants feature an atmosphere and cuisine that is not only organic and therefore healthy, but friendly to our environment as well. It strikes me that when we live in an overwhelmingly technical world, it is easy to assume we humans are in 'control' of our environment, and that perhaps if we make a 'mistake', it will be relatively easy to solve. This is a huge error. We simply cannot keep playing chemical craps with something as basic to life itself as our soil, water, and food. The ethical standard for doctors is 'Do No Harm'. The US Army uses the credo 'People First'. My own is "Serve Always, Exploit Never'. Organic farmers, it seems to me, apply all three principles in supplying us with whole, natural foods.

What does 'organic' food mean?

In the United States, 'organic' is a labeling term that describes products produced under the authority of the US Organic Foods Production Act. Organic food production means using materials and practices that enhance the ecological balance of natural systems and that integrate the parts of the farming system into an ecological whole. While organic farming practices cannot ensure that products are free of chemical residues, methods are used to minimize pollution from air, soil, and water. The primary goal of organic agriculture is to optimize the health and productivity of interdependent communities of soil, plants, animals and people.

Nora Pouillon
Chef/Owner, Restaurant Nora and Asia Nora
Author, *Cooking with Nora*

How does a restaurant become a 'certified organic' restaurant?

There must be proof that 95% of ingredients used in preparing meals are certified organic. These foods come from farms that are solely organic. There is a Certification Agency in Oregon that assesses restaurants, establishes standards, and grants credentials.

Do many restaurants serve organic food?

According to the National Restaurant Association, organic items are now offered by 57% of all restaurants with per person dinner checks of $25 or more. Over 65% of chefs surveyed indicated that they actively seek out organically grown ingredients. Organic food is now even available on airplanes, if you are flying SwissAir, that is.

NUTRITIONAL PROFILE COMPARISON

Per serving	Nutrient Rich	Old Style
calories	321	635
fat (g)	5	23
saturated fat (g)	1	7
carbohydrates (g)	48	72
fiber (g)	4	6
sodium (mg)	411	802

Where can we find organic food for our diet?

There are now more than 850 members of the Organic Trade Association in the United States, Canada, and Mexico involved in growing, processing, shipping, certifying and selling certified organic products. To find organic products in your community look for organic farmers at local farmers' markets, ask at your local health food store, check the yellow pages for organic food distributors, or contact agricultural centers at universities that often know about organic farms and community supported agriculture.

For further information on this topic contact: www.noras.com and you can order her book, *Cooking with Nora*, at 1-888-788-6672

Turkey Pot Pie

According to research studies, the typical restaurant meal has 3,000 calories, with 20% coming from carbohydrates, 40% from protein, 40% from fat. The Culinary Institute of America is promoting a shift to an 'ideal' restaurant meal of 1,000 calories (60% carbohydrate, 15% protein, 25% fat). Perhaps one day restaurants will provide two menus, one classic or old style, one nutrient rich — and, like us, print a nutritional profile to compare the two! The consumer would be able to choose wisely and eat well.

Treena and I had a great time visiting Larry Forgionne's 1776 Beekman Arms Inn in Rhinebeck, New York. The Beekman is the oldest operating inn in the United States; it is cozy, attractive, and very much an American place. A great deal of credit goes to owner/chef Larry Forgionne and his taste for the upgraded basics. He has a flair for simplification with a sophisticated and unusual twist. His pot pie is topped with a cheese biscuit and served in a shallow soup plate, a great idea and delicious. I've added one of my twists, the parsnip 'velvet' as a sauce base, so there's lots of originality here!

Main Dishes

Ingredients:

1 teaspoon non-aromatic olive oil
1/2 sweet onion, cut in 1/4" (.75 cm) dice (1 cup)
2 carrots, peeled and cut in 1/2" (1.5 cm) dice (1 cup)
2 turnips, peeled and cut in 1/2" dice
2 small parsnips, peeled and cut in 1/2"
   (1.5 cm) dice (1/2 cup)
1 1/2 cups homemade turkey
   or low sodium chicken stock
1/4 teaspoon salt
1/8 teaspoon pepper
1-pound (450 g) broccoli
2 1/2 cups cooked turkey (2/3 dark
   and 1/3 white meat)

Sauce

3/4-pound (338 g) parsnips, peeled, roughly
   chopped, and steamed until tender
1 cup evaporated skim milk
1/4 teaspoon salt

Cheese Biscuits (adapted from *Eating Well —*
   Secrets of Low-Fat Cooking)

1 cup all-purpose flour
1 cup cake flour
1 tablespoon sugar
1 1/2 teaspoons baking powder
1/2 teaspoon baking soda
1/4 teaspoon salt
1 1/2 tablespoons cold, hard, butter flavored
   margarine, cut in small pieces
3/4 cup buttermilk
1 tablespoon non-aromatic olive oil
1 tablespoon lowfat milk to brush on top
1/4 cup grated lowfat sharp cheddar cheese

Turkey Pot Pie

Serves 4

1. Heat the oil in a chef's pan or skillet on medium high, sauté the onions, carrots, turnips and parsnips on medium heat 3 minutes. Pour in the stock and season with salt and pepper. Bring to a boil, reduce the heat, cover and simmer until the vegetables are tender, 6 minutes.

2. To make the sauce: Whiz the steamed parsnips in a blender with a little of the evaporated milk until smooth, 2 minutes. Add the rest of the milk and the salt and whiz until smooth and velvety, another 30 seconds.

3. To make the biscuits:

   a. Preheat the oven to 425°F (220° C). Coat a baking sheet with pan spray. Whisk together the flours, sugar, baking powder, soda and salt in a bowl or combine in a processor.

   b. Scatter the pieces of margarine over the top and cut in with 2 knives or pulse 2 or 3 times in a processor. Make a well in the center of the dry ingredients and pour in the buttermilk and oil. Stir with a fork just until blended or pulse 2 or 3 times in the processor.

   c. Knead the dough very lightly on a floured board. Pat or roll out about 1/2" (1.5 cm) thick and cut into 4 large (3 1/2" or 9 cm) biscuits. Place on the prepared baking sheet, brush with milk, dust with cheese and bake 15 minutes or until golden.

4. While the biscuits are baking, lay the broccoli on the simmering vegetables and cook until tender, 6 minutes or until tender but still bright green. Stir in the turkey and parsnip sauce and heat through.

5. Biscuits by the nature of their chemistry are high in calories and fat. To reduce the risk, make a whole recipe, cut the tops off 4 to use in the recipe and save the bottoms and extra biscuit to toast for breakfast. Spoon the turkey mixture into 4 hot soup plates and lay the biscuit halves on top.

Cooking for All Seasons

Jimmy Schmidt, the chef and owner of a wonderful Detroit restaurant, The Rattlesnake Club, brought many 'fresh' ideas to the show while explaining his "Cooking for All Seasons' philosophy. Align your choice of ingredients with the natural cycle of seasons. There are life cycles for everything, including fruits, vegetables, fish, meats, and eggs. Foods that are in season without doubt taste best — and are best for you. They are also most bountiful, making them more available and a better value.

Jimmy Schmidt
Chef/Owner, The Rattlesnake Club
Author, *Cooking for All Seasons*

What do you mean by 'Cooking for All Seasons'?

Until modern times, we depended on the land immediately around us as our source of food without 'importing' from other climates. Our goal is to get back to depending on the earth that is close to where we live. The real 'instinctual' foods that we crave are the foods we need at different times of the year and benefit from nutritionally as well. The better the fruits and vegetables taste, the more nutritional value there generally is. We were given the ability to taste so that we could identify foods that are best for us as well as keeping us away from those foods that are less palatable and less nutritious. We all know how poorly 'imported' tomatoes taste in the winter; tomatoes in the winter have just 40% of the nutrients that they have when they have been vine-ripened.

But how do we 'Northerners' get more fresh fruits and vegetables on our table, even in the wintertime?

* In the northern climate, the late spring, summer, and autumn are wonderful seasons to go to local farmer's markets and stop at roadside farm produce stands, which helps to support the local farmer too.

* In the winter you can still get fresh produce — granted it is more limited — but there are still wonderful varieties of food including winter squashes, root vegetables, apples, pumpkins, cabbages, leeks, citrus, jicama, mangos, and papaya.

* Seasonal buying charts in the *Cooking for All Seasons Cookbook* are divided into winter, spring, summer and autumn and tell you exactly when most every fruit, vegetable, exotics, fish and shellfish, poultry and game birds, meats, wild plants and mushrooms are most available and most fresh for the absolute peak in flavor and in price.

NUTRITIONAL PROFILE COMPARISON

Per serving	Nutrient Rich	Old Style
calories	438	759
fat (g)	9	42
saturated fat (g)	2	21
carbohydrates (g)	51	41
fiber (g)	5	3
sodium (mg)	715	755

The biggest mistake that people make in the kitchen is starting off with ingredients that are not fresh.

What about finding 'fresh' herbs?

By experimenting with a variety of ingredients you are sure to find some new and wonderful flavors you have never tried before. To store herbs so they remain fresh:

* Strip them off the center core and puree them with a little white wine, roasted garlic, salt and pepper and add olive oil to it. You can keep this mixture refrigerated.

* Or, use the dry version by wrapping the herbs in muslin and hanging them in the refrigerator. This will dry the herbs and you can package them in plastic.

To learn more about 'Cooking for All Seasons' contact: The Rattlesnake Club at 313-567-4400 in Detroit, Michigan.

Hoppin' John
Atlanta, Georgia

*F*iber facts. Soluble fiber binds to fatty substances and helps to lower cholesterol as well as blood sugar levels. Insoluble fiber provides roughage, acting as a 'broom' to promote bowel regularity and colon health. So get out the fiber broom — and clean up your health!

Basically, this is 'soul' food! In its essentials, it matches many of the famed Caribbean combinations of rice and beans that have provided so many with such an excellent source of complete protein from plants. In this case, ham hocks flavor black-eyed peas and the dish of collards is spiked with lemon and hot peppers. There is something extra special about this flavorful idea . . . perhaps it's the name itself or the custom to eat this dish at New Year's, at which time the peas are for good luck and the collards for money. Perhaps the US Federal Reserve Bank should hold a New Year's Eve banquet with this as a main course . . . it certainly would do them no harm and it may just do us some good! You can substitute chipotle peppers for the ham hock if you want a 'hot' vegetarian alternative to this dish.

Main Dishes

Ingredients:

1 cup dry black eyed peas
2 pounds ham hocks
5 cups water
1 teaspoon non-aromatic olive oil
1 large sweet onion, chopped (2 cups)
3 cloves garlic, bashed and chopped
1 rib celery, chopped (1/2 cup)
4 cups stock from the ham hocks
1/2 teaspoon dried thyme
2 bay leaves
1 cup raw long grain white rice
1/8 teaspoon ground cloves
1/8 teaspoon cayenne pepper
1/4 teaspoon salt (optional)
3 heaping tablespoons chopped parsley

Collards

1/2 teaspoon non-aromatic olive oil
1/2 lemon sliced
1 dried red pepper
  or 1/8 teaspoon cayenne pepper
2 cups ham stock
8 cups washed and stemmed collard greens
1 teaspoon lemon zest
1/8 teaspoon salt
1 tablespoon lemon juice

Hoppin' John

1. Cover the black eyed peas with 3 or 4 cups of water and soak over night. To quick soak, bring to a boil, turn off the heat and let set for 1 hour. Rinse the ham hocks and cover with 8 cups water. This step can be done in a pressure cooker by cooking 30 minutes under high pressure or the old simmering way by covering and simmering 1 hour or until tender. Remove the hocks to a plate to cool and pour the stock into a fat strainer to de-fat. Set aside to use later. When the hocks are cool enough, remove and discard the skin and fat and save the meat to add at the end.

2. Heat the oil in a 10 1/2" (26.5 cm) chef's pan on medium high. Sauté the onion 3 minutes, then add the garlic to cook for 1 minute more. Stir in the celery, stock, thyme, bay leaves, rice, soaked peas, cloves, and cayenne. Bring to a boil, then reduce to simmer. Add ham hock meat and cook for 20 minutes or until the rice and peas are tender but not mushy.

3. While the beans are cooking, start the collard greens. Heat the oil in a chef's pan on medium high. Lay the lemon slices and chili pepper in the pan and cook 2 minutes. Pour in 2 cups of the de-fatted ham stock and collards, torn in roughly 2 inch pieces, and boil gently 10 minutes. Stir in the zest, salt and lemon juice and set aside until you are ready to serve.

4. When the peas are done, taste for salt and add if need be. Stir in the chopped parsley and you are ready to serve. Divide the collards among 6 hot bowls. Pour the juice left in the pan into the rice and pea mixture. Ladle the Hoppin' John onto the collards and you are ready for a real 'down home' treat!

Serves 6

Special Techniques:

Three ways to prepare beans for this dish:
1. Soak beans overnight in water until they become twice the size.
2. Cover beans with cold water and bring to a boil. Soak, off the heat, for an hour. Drain.
3. Buy canned beans, drain and rinse. (Note: this alternative may increase the sodium value significantly).

Sustainable Food Systems

There's nothing more fundamental to life that air, water, and food. Air and water problems receive considerable attention from scientists and the press, but who's explaining what we can do about the host of food problems our society faces? One person providing answers is Rod MacRae, editor of Sustainable Farming *magazine and coordinator of the Toronto Food Policy Council, who shared his knowledge about environmentally sound food systems with us on The Gathering Place.*

What are your concerns about our food?

People suspect that something is wrong with their food and the system that is producing it. Friends and family are getting sick. Food is losing its flavor. Farmers are losing their land. Giving to the food bank isn't reducing hunger in our communities. Kids are eating too much junk food. Every day a new report links food to disease. People are afraid of genetic engineering. Local food is hard to find.

Rod MacRae, PhD
Director, Food Policy Council
Editor, *Sustainable Farming*
Author, *Real Food for a Change*

What can we do?

Our approach to food has to change. It's not just about fat. People want to support local farmers and local stores. They want to socialize around food. They want their purchases to help the environment. They want their kids to grow up well nourished and free of disease. They want more natural food — 'real' food.

What do you mean by 'real' food?

Real food promotes human health. Real food is 'easy on the planet'. Real food brings people back to the table and creates joy. Real food has sustained people for centuries, foods like rice and beans.

What prevents us from eating more 'real' food?

Some people can't seem to find the time to shop for and to prepare real food. Food manufacturers and advertisers do not encourage us to eat real food. If everyone cooked natural, whole foods from scratch, there would be little profit made by food processing companies that prepare so-called 'convenience' foods.

NUTRITIONAL PROFILE COMPARISON

Per serving	Nutrient Rich	Old Style
calories	270	320
fat (g)	3	8
saturated fat (g)	1	3
carbohydrates (g)	39	50
fiber (g)	6	4
sodium (mg)	622	258

Where do we find 'real' food?

Look for organic food produced by certified organic farmers at your local farmers' market or health food store. Try more ethnic foods which are often more natural, less processed.

For further information on this topic contact: www.realfoodhome.net and read Rod MacRae's *Real Food for a Change*.

$\mathcal{B}$ishop's Lamb Stew
Vancouver, British Columbia

$\mathcal{B}$y all reasonable measures, I'm on the line between normal and, yes, overweight! How on earth, after 25 years of concentrated effort — low fat eating and speed walking — did this happen? In my case, it's been 'uneven' eating at odd times during many travels in multiple time zones. Try to even out your meals, eat at planned times and in smaller quantities — even if your are not 'galloping' like me.

One of the greatest pleasures I have is to meet fellow professionals for whom I have both a deep respect and a genuine liking. John Bishop, the chef-owner of Vancouver's 'Bishops', is just such a man. For over 15 years he has diligently, delicately, and deliciously served his clientele with simply great food, in perhaps one of the worlds' most elegant small dining rooms. In so doing, he has won countless awards and deserves every one of them. This comfort food dish of lamb with rosemary dumplings will introduce you to a man whose book, Cooking at My House, contains this very special dish.

Main Dishes

Ingredients:

2 1/2 pounds (1.25 kg) lamb shoulder steaks
1 teaspoon non-aromatic olive oil
1/2 large onion, chopped (1 cup)
2 cloves garlic, bashed and chopped
1 fennel bulb, trimmed
  and cut in 1" (2.5 cm) dice
1 1/2 cups celery, cut in 1" (2.5 cm) dice
1 1/2 cups carrots, cut in 1" (2 .5 cm) rounds
2 tablespoons tomato paste
1 cup de-alcoholized red wine
1/4 teaspoon freshly ground black pepper
1/4 teaspoon salt
3 cups lamb or low sodium homemade or
  canned chicken stock (see 'The Basics')
1 tablespoon arrowroot mixed with 1/4 cup
  red wine (slurry)

Rosemary Dumplings
1 cup flour
1 teaspoon baking powder
1 teaspoon finely chopped rosemary,
  fresh or dried
1/4 teaspoon salt
1 tablespoon extra virgin olive oil
1/2 cup 1% milk

Bishop's Lamb Stew with Rosemary Dumplings

1. Preheat the oven to 375°F (190°C). Trim fat and bone from the lamb steaks. You should have 1-1/4 pounds (565 g) of lean meat. Cut in 2" (5 cm) chunks. There will be lots of trim from which you can make a nice rich stock. See 'The Basics' for instructions.

2. Heat the oil in a chef's pan or large skillet on medium high. When it's nice and hot, add the pieces of lamb in one layer on the bottom. Brown on one side, about 5 minutes. Remove to a plate and set aside.

3. Return the pan to the heat and add the onions. Cook 1 minute then stir in the garlic, fennel, celery, and carrots. Sauté for 2 minutes or until the onion starts to wilt. Pull the vegetables to the side of the pan and add the tomato paste. Stir the paste until it darkens, 2 minutes, then combine with the vegetables. De-glaze the pan with the wine, scraping the brown flavorful bits off the bottom. Add the reserved meat, pepper and salt. Pour in the stock, bring to a boil, cover and bake in the preheated oven 1 hour.

4. Just before the stew is done, start the dumplings. Combine the flour, baking powder, rosemary and salt in a bowl. Add the oil to the milk and pour into the flour mixture. Mix gently with a fork to make a soft dough. Divide the dough into 6 pieces. Lay the dumplings on top of the stew, cover again and bake 15 more minutes or until the dumplings are done.

5. To finish the stew, pull the dumplings to the side of the pan on a burner set at medium high. Stir the slurry into the liquid. It will thicken almost immediately. Serve on hot plates with a green vegetable such as lightly steamed baby bok choy.

Serves 6

Dining Table Ambiance

The motto 'good food in good taste' can be applied not only to the food we eat but also to the atmosphere we create at the dining table. Creating a warm environment does not have to take a lot of time. Be thoughtful in the process of meal preparation and table setting. You are sure to have fun and bring a lot of joy to those you serve. Here are some hints from John Bishop for making dinner heartwarming as well as heart healthy!

How can we create a pleasant ambiance for dining?

* Use a nice napkin (paper or cloth).
* Place fresh herbs from the garden or fresh flowers on the table.
* Find artifacts for the table — pottery, silver, and other special pieces create a more interesting table.
* Warm the plates for hot food, which will help to keep the food warm throughout the meal.
* Serving food buffet-style can eliminate the stress of having to plate all the food, so everyone can gather at the table and enjoy the food together.

John Bishop, CCP
Chef/Owner, Bishops
Author, *Cooking at My House*

What else can you suggest for creating a 'home' feel at the table?

Healthy homestyle cooking does not necessarily require a lot of time and a lot of ingredients. Simple sauces can take just a few minutes, yet still lend a hand-crafted feel/flavor. By using simple and nourishing ingredients, you can create a meal that comforts and satisfies. You can easily create an environment in which guests will enjoy 'nurturing' food and a heartwarming experience in the comfort of your own home.

For further information on this topic, read John Bishop's *Cooking at My House*.

NUTRITIONAL PROFILE COMPARISON

Per serving	Nutrient Rich	Old Style
calories	350	360
fat (g)	10	16
saturated fat (g)	3	4
carbohydrates (g)	29	22
fiber (g)	3	2
sodium (mg)	420	806

Develop an appreciation for a variety
of ingredients — and take the time
to enjoy the table.

Turkey Picadillo & Cuban Black Beans

Miami, Florida

Body fat is our final defense in a famine. Starve the body with less than 1,200-1,400 calories a day and the body will draw on lean muscle before it draws on fat resources. Remember, you must exercise to build muscle, ideally a combination of aerobic and strength building exercises. Nobody wants to be a bunch of bones gathered up in sagging, fatty tissue! Work hard to develop your muscles. You'll look and feel much better.

Nothing is quite so comforting as good Cuban food-of-the-people; it's simple, well flavored, and designed to feed working men and women with the very fruits of their labors. Unfortunately, it has not been directly translated (within reason) to our North American plates. With close to 1,000 calories and 47 grams of fat, it is too much for our more sedentary lifestyles. In this case, my guest Thais Correno, from her cantina service in Miami, has made great strides both personally and professionally to lower the risks without spoiling the traditional ethnic flavors or the feeling of satisfaction.

Main Dishes

Ingredients:

Sofrito
4 cups roughly chopped sweet onions
1 large green bell pepper, roughly chopped
7 cloves garlic
1 tablespoon distilled vinegar

Picadillo
1 teaspoon non-aromatic olive oil, divided
1 teaspoon ground cumin
1 tablespoon tomato paste
1 1/2-pounds (675 g) extra lean ground turkey
1/4 teaspoon salt
1 tablespoon capers
10 large black olives
2 tablespoons raisins
2 tablespoons fine sliced cilantro
3 cups boiled white or brown rice (optional)

Cuban Black Beans
1 teaspoon non-aromatic olive oil
1/4 cup sofrito
1 teaspoon cumin
1 teaspoon brown sugar
1 tablespoon vinegar
2 cups home cooked or canned black beans, drained and rinsed
1 1/2 cups dealcoholized dry white wine
4 bay leaves
1/4 teaspoon salt

Baked Plantains
2 ripe plantains

Turkey Picadillo and Cuban Black Beans

1. To make the sofrito, place the onions, peppers, garlic and vinegar in a blender. Start the blender at the chop level then increase speed to puree. Whiz until smooth. This will keep in the refrigerator for a week and can be used to add flavor to soups, stews, and casseroles.

2. Heat 1/2 teaspoon of the oil in a skillet or chef's pan on medium high. Sauté 3 tablespoons of the sofrito, 1 tablespoon of the tomato paste and the cumin together until the mix is thick and dark. Reserve on a plate and rinse the pan.

3. Heat the remaining 1/2 teaspoon oil and brown the turkey, mashing it as you go to keep it loose. Stir in the salt, remaining sofrito, and tomato paste along with the capers, olives and raisins. Serve over rice with Cuban Black Beans and baked plantain for a comforting Cuban meal. It will look fresh and interesting if you scatter everything with fine sliced cilantro.

Cuban Black Beans

1. Heat the oil in a chef's pan or large saucepan on medium high. Fry the sofrito and cumin, stirring, 2 minutes. Add the sugar, vinegar, beans, wine, bay and salt. Simmer until thick, about 25 minutes.

2. Serve with the picadillo.

Baked Plantains

Preheat the oven to 375°F (190°C). Slit the skin of 2 ripe plantains from end to end. Lay in a baking dish slit side up and bake 1 hour or until tender. Peel, slice on the diagonal and serve with the picadillo and beans.

Serves 6

Healthy Latin Cooking

From our guest Thais Carreno, we have seen that with few resources yet a wealth of passion just one individual can work wonders with her native cuisine and the health of those she cooks for. Changes can be made, health can be achieved, and food can be enjoyed. Hang on to your native cuisine, to the foods that define who you are, then make them a bit healthier so that you can live longer — and happier! Just look at the numbers to see what Thais and I did with her turkey picadillo.

What inspired you to create low-fat Cuban food?

One day I realized that I was only 5'2" tall and weighed 202 pounds, and after having my children. I also have a strong family history of heart disease and diabetes on both sides of the family. I wanted to live long enough to raise my children. Additionally, I love cooking and have a natural love for food as an art. I wanted to be able to eat from my gastronomical roots without putting my health in jeopardy.

Thais Carreno
Owner, Fat Busters Cantina Service

What is Cuban cooking?

It draws most of its influence from Spain and the Canary Islands. 'Sofrito' is the key to flavorful Latin food, a combination of onions, garlic, sweet peppers, vinegar, as well as various spices and fresh herbs. You don't need to have fat to make it taste good.

How does Fat Busters Cantina Service work?

Fat Busters is a personalized, low-fat food catering or 'cantina' service (cowboys carried their food in a three-section container or canteen). For $39.92 per week (Monday-Friday), we provide one entrée and three side orders daily. We also serve food by the pound as well. The menu includes rice, beans, picadillo, jerk chicken with a Cuban twist, oven baked barbecue turkey, and other Cuban dishes. We serve 350-400 meals a day. About 60% of Fat Busters clientele are Latin, mostly elderly, but a younger group of customers is growing.

For further information on this topic contact: www.Cubanlite@aol.com

NUTRITIONAL PROFILE COMPARISON

Per serving	Nutrient Rich	Old Style
calories	302	948
fat (g)	4	47
saturated fat (g)	1	12
carbohydrates (g)	38	95
fiber (g)	8	15
sodium (mg)	197	676

abbit Pie

St John's, Newfoundland

The 65 and older population is growing at a rapid rate! In fact, it will increase by 62% in the United States over the next two decades, to 53.3 million from 33 million. It's never too late to begin to move more to improve your health and to lift your spirits.

This pie is just plain delicious! I'm tempted to tell you that you can substitute either chicken or turkey thighs for the rabbit. However, whilst they will do well, there is something quite wonderful about rabbit, fennel, and a hint of wild mushrooms cooked in red 'wine' that should not be missed. Better to order the rabbit with your meat market and plan ahead for an weekend evening treat for the family.

Main Dishes

Ingredients:

1 recipe Graham's Basic Pie Crust
   (see 'The Basics')
2 fennel bulbs, trimmed
   and cut in thick slices
1 tablespoon freshly squeezed lemon juice
1/2 -pound (225 g) medium mushrooms,
   halved
2 teaspoons dried mushroom powder
1 1/2 teaspoons non-aromatic olive oil,
   divided
1/2 cup flour
1/4 teaspoon salt
1/4 teaspoon pepper
1 rabbit, cut into pieces
1 onion, cut in 1/4" (.75-cm) dice (2 cups)
3 cloves garlic, bashed and chopped
2 carrots, peeled and cut on the diagonal in
   1/2" (1.5-cm) pieces (1 1/2 cups)
2 ribs celery, cut in 1/2" (1.5-cm) slices
   (generous cup)
2 tablespoons tomato paste
2 cups de-alcoholized red wine
1/4 teaspoon salt
1/4 teaspoon pepper
8 big fresh sage leaves or 2 teaspoons
   powdered sage
4 4-inch (10-cm) sprigs rosemary or
   1 tablespoon dried

Rabbit Pie

1. Steam the fennel slices for 10 minutes. Preheat oven to 350°F (180°C). Lay the slices of steamed fennel in the bottom of a greased 9" x 13" (23 x 33 cm) baking dish or large oval baker. Heat in a skillet on medium high. Pour the lemon juice into the hot pan and add the mushrooms. Cook until browned and tender, stirring often. Stir in the mushroom powder and scatter over the fennel in the baking dish.

2. Reheat the pan on medium and add 1 teaspoon of the oil. Combine the flour, salt and pepper in a bag. Shake the rabbit pieces in the flour until covered and tap off excess. Brown on both sides in the hot pan. Remove to a plate and set aside.

3. Pour the remaining 1/2 teaspoon oil and sauté the onions in the same pan for 2 minutes, then add the garlic, carrots and celery and cook 2 or 3 minutes more. Pull the vegetables to the side and add the tomato paste. Cook, mixing with the vegetables until the tomato paste darkens and coats all the vegetables. Pour in the wine and season with salt, pepper, sage, and rosemary. Lay the browned rabbit on top, cover and bring to a boil. Place in the preheated oven and bake 30 to 40 minutes or until the rabbit is tender but not falling off the bone.

4. Remove the rabbit to a plate to cool a bit. Increase the oven heat to 425°F (220°C). Take the meat off the bones in large pieces and lay on top of the mushrooms in the baking dish. Pour the baking liquid and vegetables over the top. Roll out the pie crust to fit the pan. Pinch the crust around the edges and prick the center with a fork. Brush the top with a little whole or 2% milk. Bake 15 or 20 minutes or until golden. Cut into 8 pieces and serve. Steamed broccoli and carrots would make up a really attractive plate.

Serves 8

Special Techniques:

* Dried mushrooms can be ground to a fine powder by placing them into a spice or coffee mill; this flavorful powder will add a wealth of flavor to any dish.
* Tomato paste can be added to some casseroles and sautéed with the accompanying vegetables for depth of flavor and a smoky hint to the dish.

Exercising Seniors

It is never too late to start exercising; the older you are the more important it is to be active! This is the message Steve Nelson brought to The Gathering Place when we invited him to talk about the 'SilverSneakers' fitness program for seniors.

What are the benefits of regular exercise for seniors?

1. Exercise has a dramatic effect on a wealth of different ailments, reducing, for example, coronary artery disease risk, hypertension, and arthritis symptoms.

2. Exercise improves physical and mental well-being significantly. It has been shown that people who exercise have better health behaviors. Exercise can heighten and increase many aspects of your health, including bone density, mobility, lung capacity, muscle mass and tone, strength, flexibility and endurance.

3. Most importantly, total body-conditioning classes, like SilverSneakers, provide an avenue for seniors to be more independent and do simple day-to-day tasks while making friends at the same time.

Steve Nelson, MBA, MHCA
Former Senior Vice-President, Healthcare Dimensions

How does SilverSneakers work?

Health Care Dimensions is a company that specializes in providing preventive health care solutions for seniors: Out of this effort flourished an innovative approach to providing fitness programs for seniors called SilverSneakers. The program allows seniors with a given health plan/insurance company to have access to many of the fitness facilities within their local area with full membership privileges and to participate in related health programs, including nutrition programs, free of charge. All of the instructors and health educators have common training and teach the same information. The various programs can be tailored to the readiness and fitness levels of individuals. The key to the SilverSneakers programs throughout the country is that the core science is the same in each facility.

NUTRITIONAL PROFILE COMPARISON

Per serving	Nutrient Rich	Old Style
calories	355	571
fat (g)	13	27
saturated fat (g)	3	12
carbohydrates (g)	28	42
fiber (g)	2	6
sodium (mg)	280	809

How can we get involved with a local SilverSneakers or similar program?

1. First, log onto the website to see if SilverSneakers is available in your area.
2. If SilverSneakers is not in your vicinity, call your health plan/insurance company at the highest level you can reach, to ask for the program to be implemented in your community.
3. In the meantime, search for a qualified exercise physiologist who can draw up an exercise plan that meets your needs and considers your own health concerns.
4. Always make sure you begin any exercise program with your physician's approval.

For more information contact: www.silversneakers.com or www.hcdimensions.com or 1- 800-295-4993

Chicken Enchiladas
Scottsdale, Arizona

There is a whole wide world out there offering a vast array of different yet delicious cuisines which are often full of fresh, whole, nutritious foods. Broaden your horizons with food choices you make. Experiment with the many international and multicultural cuisines, flavors, and foods that are just a restaurant or a cookbook away.

When we were living in England (until 1958), in New Zealand (until 1964), in Australia (until 1969), and in Canada (until 1971), we were never exposed to really good Mexican cooking. This has now changed since our arrival in the United States in 1974. Every year, thanks to experts like Diana Kennedy and Rick Bayless, we have seen increasingly well-made dishes, especially when 'tweaked' to bring lard levels into line with our much lower calorie intakes in America. Here is an example of a good modern enchilada.

Main Dishes

Ingredients:

Sauce
1/2 teaspoon non-aromatic olive oil
1/2 cup roughly chopped onions
1 clove garlic, bashed and chopped
1 jalapeno chili, seeded and chopped
1/4 teaspoon cayenne pepper (optional)
1 teaspoon ground cumin
1-pound (450 g) Roma tomatoes, peeled and
  roughly chopped
1 can , 10 3/4-ounce (310 g), tomato puree
1 teaspoon dried oregano
1 1/2 cups canned or homemade low sodium
  chicken stock (see 'The Basics')

Filling
8-ounce boned, skin on chicken breast
1 cup canned or homemade low sodium
  chicken stock (see 'The Basics')
1/2 cup low fat cottage cheese
1/4 cup low fat yogurt
2 tablespoons chopped cilantro
2 teaspoons cornstarch
8 5" (13 cm) flour tortillas (cut larger ones to
  size if necessary)
4 whole canned mild green chilies, cut
  lengthwise into 1/2" (1 1/2 cm) strips
1/4 cup finely chopped onion
1/2 cup low fat Monterey jack cheese

Chicken Enchiladas

1. Preheat the oven to 350°F (180°C). Heat the oil in a skillet or saucepan on medium high. Sauté the onion 2 minutes, add the garlic, jalapeno, optional cayenne, and cumin and cook 2 minutes more. Stir in the tomatoes, tomato puree, and oregano. Whiz in a blender or processor then add the chicken stock. Bring to a boil, reduce the heat and simmer 20 minutes.

2. Place the chicken breast, skin side up, in a small skillet. Add the stock and cover with a piece of waxed paper cut to size. Bring to a boil, reduce the heat, and poach very gently 20 minutes. Cool, remove the skin, and cut across the grain in thin slices. It may still be a little pink inside, but will finish cooking when the enchiladas are baked.

3. Whiz the cottage cheese until smooth in a blender or processor. Add the yogurt, cilantro, and cornstarch and pulse to mix.

4. Spoon a little of the tomato sauce into a 9" x 13" (23 x 33 cm) baking dish. Dip a tortilla into the sauce and lay on a plate. Spread a tablespoon of the cottage cheese mixture down the center. Lay pieces of chicken and green chilies on top and sprinkle with a little chopped onion. Roll and lay in the prepared baking dish. Repeat with the rest of the ingredients. Cover with the remaining tomato sauce, scatter the grated cheese on top, and bake in the preheated oven 20 minutes or until heated through.

Serves 4

Vegetarian Option: Chicken Enchiladas

Replace the chicken stock in the sauce with low sodium vegetable broth. Instead of chicken, spread 2 tablespoons canned or homemade vegetarian refried beans on the cottage cheese mixture and make the enchiladas as above.

International Food Guidelines

From Professor Marcia Magnus we learned that different nations have different health profiles and food guides. From the food guides developed in other countries we can not only enjoy greater variety in our diet but also see possible ways of preventing disease. The primary goal of food guides is to communicate an optimal diet for overall health of the population. Food guides are used to improve quality of life and nutritional well-being in a simplified and understandable way. So, being cosmopolitan or global in our outlook on food may be as 'profitable' as going global is in business.

What are 'health profiles' and 'dietary guidelines'?

The health profile of a population is different in each country and therefore results in dietary guidelines being different as well. The purpose of these guides is to demonstrate appropriate eating behavior.

1. In industrialized countries heart disease and cancer are the primary fatal diseases and health concerns, while in the developing countries, there is an increasing rate of heart disease and cancer, but life expectancy is in the 40-50 years of age range and a major cause of death is motor accidents.
2. Food guides in developed countries tend to promote a diet that prevents chronic disease, while food guides in underdeveloped countries promote a diet that provides nutrients to safeguard against malnutrition.

What do we find in common among the various international food guides?

* Variety of foods (balance) and a concern for the amount of food eaten (reasonable portions) are shared concerns.
* All international food guides are carbohydrate based, with breads, cereals, and grains emphasized as the largest part of the diet for the benefit of health.

How can we incorporate more variety into our diet?

You need to be brave and willing to try new foods. Experiment with new restaurants that prepare various ethnic foods. Look for festivals and events that serve food where you can

Marcia Magnus, PhD
Associate Professor, International Nutrition, Florida International University

NUTRITIONAL PROFILE COMPARISON

Per serving	Nutrient Rich	Vegetarian	Old Style
calories	375	337	1019
fat (g)	9	8	57
saturated fat (g)	2	2	32
carbohydrates (g)	44	49	58
fiber (g)	6	7	9
sodium (mg)	622	729	1373

try popular ethnic foods (for example, the Chinese New Year Festival). Invest yourself in a search for great International dishes.

For further information on this topic contact: www.ificinfo.health.org

From the Japanese Food Guide: 'Happy eating makes for happy family life. Sit down and eat together and talk. Treasure family taste and home cooking.'

New England Boiled Dinner

Portland, Maine

We use sodium chloride (table salt), sodium glutamate (MSG), and other sodium (phosphate, ascorbate, bicarbonate) to prepare, season, and preserve our food. But consuming too much sodium can be dangerous, triggering the body to retain fluids, thus increasing the volume of the blood vessels, resulting in 'high' pressure being placed on the artery walls as the heart beats. Roughly one in every four of us in the so-called 'developed' world has high blood pressure. Of this number, somewhere between 30-50% are described as 'salt' or sodium sensitive. Moderate the use of sodium in your diet to about 2,400 mg per day — or less.

Much depends upon getting a good piece of corned beef brisket when preparing this classic comfort food. In the 'old days', you could trust your butcher to have his very own 'select' recipe and the result was almost heaven. Nowadays, we can buy it ready packed in 'cryovac' — some brands are good, others disappointing. The answer is to find a good one and stay with it. By all means, do trim off any excess fat. This is really wonderful eating — only a good mustard needs to be added (I'll leave you to select your favorite!) The nutritional 'numbers' — especially the sodium and fat content — improve because of the reversed roles of meat to vegetables and the de-fatted 'soup'.

New England Boiled Dinner

Ingredients:

Meat

2 1/2 -pounds (1.25-k) lean corned beef
   brisket
4 bay leaves
1/2 teaspoon black peppercorns
1/2 teaspoon mustard seeds
4 whole cloves
4 allspice berries

Vegetables

1-pound (0.5-k) carrots, peeled, cut in half
   lengthwise and crosswise
12-ounces (340-g) parsnips, peeled, thick part
   cut in half, thin part left whole
12-ounces (340-g) rutabagas, peeled, cut in
   1/2" (11/2 -cm) x 3" (8-cm) sticks
12 tiny red potatoes cut in half
18 small onions, peeled (1 inch or 3 cm
   diameter)
1 small head cabbage cut in 6ths
2 tablespoons chopped parsley

1. Cover the corned beef with water in a large Dutch oven. Add the bay, peppercorns, mustard seeds, cloves, and allspice berries and bring to a boil. (For extra flavor, add a good handful of the peelings from the vegetables to the water.) Reduce the heat and simmer 2 hours or until the meat is tender but not falling apart.

2. Remove the meat, strain and de-fat the liquid. Return the meat and fat free liquid to the pan. Add carrots, parsnips, rutabagas, potatoes, and onions, and bring to a boil. Cook 20 minutes or until tender. The cabbage wedges can be steamed on top of the other vegetables if you have a steamer to fit your pan, or steamed separately 15 minutes or until tender.

3. Slice the meat across the grain in 1/2" (1.5 cm) slices and divide among 6 hot soup plates. Arrange the vegetables around the meat and pour a little of the liquid over the top. Sprinkle with chopped parsley and serve with mustard.

Serves 6

Heart Health

Heart disease does affect everyone since 50% of us will suffer from the disease direct-ly while the rest of us will know family members, friends, and colleagues who have 'heart' health problems. The risk of heart disease, even in a healthy person, is much greater than any other disease. Because we are an aging society, these rates will probably climb, unless we change our lifestyle. I can't think of a better reason to become more reasonable in the way we eat and exercise. Dr Barry Effron, Chief of Cardiology at University Hospitals of Cleveland, offers us some highly reasonable ways of doing so.

Is heart disease preventable?

Ninety percent of heart disease is preventable because most heart disease is due to six 'environmental' risk factors that can be controlled.

1. Smoking
2. Overweight
3. High blood pressure
4. High cholesterol
5. High triglycerides
6. Lack of exercise

If you have one risk factor, you have double or even triple the risk for heart disease com-pared with someone who has no risk factors, and once you start adding risk factors (three or more), your risk is ten times greater . . . and with four or five risk factors, it will be clos-er to 20 times greater the risk than someone who has no risk factors at all.

What can we do to reduce our risk of heart disease?

1. Stop smoking — complete abstinence is critical.
2. For those with high blood pressure, you must lower it! If necessary, take medication that will lower your blood pressure to the normal range. If above 140/90, it will be nec-essary for a physician to work with you to employ the following health strategies: diet, exercise, and probably medication.
3. Diabetes (enormous risk factor) must be diligently controlled.

Barry Effron, MD
Associate Chief, Cardiology,
University Hospitals of Cleveland
Associate Professor, Case Western Reserve
University School of Medicine

NUTRITIONAL PROFILE COMPARISON

Per serving	Nutrient Rich	Old Style
calories	379	617
fat (g)	8	26
saturated fat (g)	3	8
carbohydrates (g)	60	68
fiber (g)	8	14
sodium (mg)	683	1622

Heart Disease can be largely prevented with lifestyle changes and medication. Even when people have heart disease, the risk can be greatly modified with careful attention to risk factors. With this effort, we can enjoy more 'quality' years.

4. Start exercising. Fifty percent of individuals don't exercise at all, and only 10-15% of people exercise to the point that it is beneficial for cardiovascular health. All you need to do is walk 30 minutes a day most days of the week (3 miles per hour). There is a 30-50 percent reduction of long-term heart risk with regular exercise.

5. Know what your cholesterol level is by having a full lipid profile. This test includes a Total cholesterol value, HDL, LDL and triglycerides. To lower cholesterol you can modify diet, and may need to take medication along with a physician's help, which can lead to a risk reduction of 33% or more.

6. Aspirin is a key preventive strategy for heart disease. Research has shown that men over age 45 and women over age 55 with other risk factors who take 1 baby aspirin or 1/2 aspirin a day will reduce the risk of heart disease by up to 25%, long-term.

For further information on this topic contact: www.UHHS.com or www.americanheart.org

exas Chili

Houston, Texas

Chocolate is my Achilles' heel! For years I agonized over a way of cutting chocolate from my diet in my effort to live within 'reason'. But sometimes passion simply overwhelms reason. With a sigh of relief, I learned from one of our Gathering Place guests that chocolate, eaten in moderation, is not a dietary sin. I can now enjoy chocolate within reason — not just in desserts but also in chili!

It seems entirely reasonable that a man with an accent like mine could present a credibility gap when it comes to the development of a 'Texas Chili' (said with a distinct drawl). Let it be said that I've been there, and even got chili stains on my t-shirt! This is a delicious combination of many genuine Texas ideas. When you try it, please do try the raw garlic and please don't leave out the cocoa! The addition of red wine adds color, depth of flavor and originality . . . perhaps even the hint of an accent?

Main Dishes

Ingredients:

1 1/2 teaspoons non-aromatic olive oil,
 divided
8-ounces (227-g) bottom round,
 cut in fine dice
8-ounces (227-g) turkey thigh, cut in fine dice
1 onion, cut into 1/4" (.75 cm) dice
10 3/4-ounce (305-g) can tomato puree
2 jalapeno peppers, seeded and chopped
 (leave the seeds if you like it hot)
1 can (4-ounce) diced green chilies
1 teaspoon ground cumin
1 teaspoon dried oregano
1/4 teaspoon cayenne pepper
1 tablespoon cocoa
1/4 teaspoon salt
1 1/2 cups de-alcoholized red wine (this is an
 option, can be replaced with beef stock)
1 1/2 cups canned or homemade low sodium
 beef stock or water (see 'The Basics')
3 cloves garlic, bashed and chopped
1 tablespoon cornmeal
1 1/2 cups cooked brown rice
3 cups canned pinto beans,
 rinsed and drained

Garnish
1/2 cup finely chopped raw onions
1/2 cup chopped cilantro
6 tablespoons parmesan cheese

Texas Chili

1. Mix 1 teaspoon of the oil with the diced beef. Drop into a hot pan to brown. When it's pretty well browned, about 2 minutes, add the turkey and continue cooking 2 more minutes. Tip out onto a plate.

2. Heat the remaining oil in the unwashed pan and sauté the onion until it starts to wilt, 2 to 3 minutes. Add the tomato puree, jalapenos, diced chiles, cumin, oregano, cayenne, cocoa, and salt. Cook 1 minute longer. Pour in the wine and stock, bring to a boil, reduce the heat and simmer 30 minutes.

3. Stir in the garlic and cornmeal. Cook 3 or 4 minutes until the chili thickens. Divide the rice and beans among 6 hot bowls. Ladle the chili over the top and pass the garnishes at the table.

Serves 6

The Mystique of Chocolate

Research has proven that there are no harmful effects from chocolate when consumed as part of a healthy and well-balanced diet. Chocolate has various properties that make it a desirable and pleasurable food as experienced by those who actually 'crave chocolate', as well as those who eat chocolate just because they enjoy it. Chocolate will continue to be enjoyed by many as an ending to a meal, a token of love, or for a festive occasion — and someday may even be enjoyed because of its relationship to health. Something this good can't be bad for you!

Why do we crave chocolate?

Some people really do suffer from chocolate cravings, experiencing a sense of withdrawal. Research shows that 15-20% of women get chocolate cravings. It is likely that we crave the combination of fat, sugar, and texture. Chocolate may affect neurotransmitters in the brain, making us feel better. In addition, our childhood pleasure in chocolate as a treat may be an emotional factor.

Douglas L. Taren, PhD
Associate Professor, Arizona Prevention Center,
University of Arizona College of Medicine

What are the nutritional components of chocolate?

* Sugar.
* Fat: the majority of fat is stearic acid, which has a neutral effect on blood cholesterol, neither raising it nor lowering it.
* Antioxidants/phytochemicals, specifically polyphenols: these are compounds with health-benefiting properties found in plant-based foods that may promote heart health.

What is an appropriate or 'reasonable' serving of chocolate?

1 oz. — and this is important to keep in mind! Proper portion size makes it feasible to understand moderation and therefore fit chocolate into a healthy diet. If you consume greater portions frequently, you may find it difficult to maintain an ideal weight

Are there health benefits to consuming chocolate or should we avoid it?

* There may be a link between people who eat chocolate and those who live longer according to data from a physicians' health study. There is additional data that shows

NUTRITIONAL PROFILE COMPARISON

Per serving	Nutrient Rich	Old Style
calories	377	664
fat (g)	8	34
saturated fat (g)	2	11
carbohydrates (g)	43	42
fiber (g)	8	13
sodium (mg)	877	1772

those who report eating chocolate live longer. Researchers are also studying the antioxidant properties of chocolate.

* If you are faced with a weight problem and would like to control your calorie intake, then you may want to eliminate chocolate from your diet.

* However, if it is not causing weight problems and you use it in moderation, it can be a very appropriate part of the diet.

* There are no substitutes that will give you the same effect on mood as chocolate, so it is imperative to sit down with a registered dietitian to find out how to have a healthy diet that incorporates chocolate.

For more information on this topic: Contact: www.chocolateinfo.com

Boston Cream Pie

Boston, Massachusetts

Some recent fad diets have given carbohydrates a bad reputation. But if you have ever thought about eliminating carbohydrates from your diet, remember this . . . if you take out a whole food group like carbohydrates, there will be a great imbalance that takes place. There is not any one food that can give us everything we need. Diets that suggest we can eliminate carbohydrates totally are not well balanced, and therefore can't possibly be a long-term alternative for healthy living.

Nobody, it seems, knows why this cake is called a pie. Perhaps it was yet another import from England, where it had been known as a 'pudding cake pie', again for no apparent reason. When the famous Parker House Hotel opened in Boston late in 1855, they converted the cake slightly by adding a 'thin' chocolate glaze that keeps on running over the edges of the whole cake and slices. They renamed it Boston Cream Pie. Once again, a few changes bring this classic up to date: no butter in the cake, a filling of lower fat (not non fat) vanilla yogurt cheese sweetened with maple syrup and textured with toasted, sliced almonds, and the chocolate glaze now has coffee and cocoa. It is, by the way, delicious and cuts 200 calories and 17 grams of fat per slice off the original.

Desserts

Ingredients:

Sponge Cake
1/3 cup sifted cake flour
3 tablespoons cornstarch
3 large eggs at room temperature
3 large egg whites at room temperature
1 teaspoon non-aromatic olive oil
1 teaspoon vanilla extract
1/2 cup + 1 tablespoon granulated sugar
1/2 teaspoon cream of tartar

Filling
1 cup vanilla low fat yogurt cheese
  (see 'The Basics')
1 tablespoon maple syrup
1/3 cup toasted sliced almonds

Chocolate Glaze
1 cup powdered sugar
3 tablespoons Dutch cocoa
3 tablespoons strong coffee
1/2 teaspoon vanilla

Boston Cream Pie

1. Preheat the oven to 425°F (220°C). Spray two 9″ (23 cm) cake pans. Cut parchment or wax paper to fit the bottom of each, spray and dust with flour.

2. Combine the flour and cornstarch in a small bowl. Using 2 mixing bowls, place the 3 egg whites in one and 2 of the whole eggs in the other. Separate the third egg and put the yolk with the whole eggs and the white with the whites, where you now have 4 egg whites. Add the oil, vanilla, and 1/2 cup of the sugar to the whole eggs and beat for a full 5 minutes. The mixture will be thick and creamy. Fold in the flour mixture half at a time. The more you manipulate batter, the tougher and less tender your product will be.

3. Beat the egg whites, adding the cream of tartar when foamy. Add the remaining tablespoon of sugar when soft peaks form and continue beating until stiff and shiny. Spoon 1/4 of the beaten whites into the batter and stir to lighten. Fold in the rest. Divide between the 2 prepared pans. Bake for 6 minutes in the preheated oven or until set and golden in color. Cool for 10 minutes on a rack then loosen and remove from the pans to cool completely.

4. While the cake is cooling, make the filling and the glaze. Stir the yogurt cheese and maple syrup together and mix thoroughly to make the filling. Combine the powdered sugar, cocoa, coffee, and vanilla in a small bowl for the glaze. Cover so it doesn't form a crust.

5. To assemble the 'pie', lay one of the cake layers on a serving plate. Cover with the filling and scattered toasted almonds. Lay the second cake layer on top. Drizzle on the glaze starting in the center. Try to keep most of it on top of the cake so when you cut it, the glaze will dribble attractively down the sides of each wedge.

Serves 8

Special Techniques:

* Preparing cake pans: Trace the cake pan on wax paper and place the cut-out rounds inside the cake pans, spray each with oil spray, and drop a tablespoon of flour and spread around the oiled pans. Shake off the excess.

Carbohydrate Facts

Registered dietitian Leslie Bonci dropped by The Gathering Place to provide us with the hard facts about carbohydrates, that much maligned food group. Carbohydrates are the highest quality of fuel available for working, growing bodies. They are the cornerstone of a disease prevention diet. When chosen properly, foods rich in carbohydrates are also rich in vitamins, minerals, fiber and phytochemicals that are essential to great health. Neglect them at your peril.

Could you define carbohydrates for us?

Carbohydrates are macronutrients that come in two primary forms:
1. Simple carbohydrates are available from raw or refined sugars in juices, sodas, candy, and desserts.
   * No more than 20% of our carbohydrate consumption should be in this form.
   * You can have simple carbohydrates in your diet, just keep them limited since they are often void of nutrition.
   * 'Sweet' is one of the primary taste buds in our mouth, and if we avoid these foods, often times we will later crave sweets and might overindulge.

2. Complex carbohydrates are available from whole grains, vegetables, beans, potatoes, pastas and breads.
   * 80% of our intake of carbohydrates should come on this form.
   * Complex carbohydrates provide a large amount of vitamins, minerals, and phytonutrients required for good health.
   * The majority of fiber in our diet comes from complex carbohydrate sources. Fiber helps to keep the gut healthy, and may help to lower heart disease and cancer risk.

How much carbohydrate should we consume?

1. Total Carbohydrate:
   To estimate your carbohydrate needs, multiply your weight x 3 to calculate carbohydrate grams needed each day. If weight loss is your goal, you may want to decrease this number.

Leslie Bonci, MPH, RD
Director, Sports Medicine Nutrition,
Department of Orthopedic Surgery & Center for Sports Medicine,
University of Pittsburgh Medical Center
Spokesperson, American Dietetic Association

NUTRITIONAL PROFILE COMPARISON

Per serving	Nutrient Rich	Old Style
calories	249	449
fat (g)	3	20
saturated fat (g)	1	11
carbohydrates (g)	48	60
fiber (g)	1	2
sodium (mg)	86	269

2. Simple vs Complex Carbohydrates:nnn
   If you consume 400 grams of carbohydrate in one day, no more than 80 grams should come from sugars (20% of total carbohydrate). The rest should be in the form of complex sources.
3. Fiber:
   * For adults, the goal for fiber is 20-25 grams a day, though most people eat only 8-10 grams a day.
   * For children ages 2-18, calculate their fiber needs in grams by taking their age and adding 5.

How can we make carbohydrates part of our meal planning?

* When you plan your meals, aim to serve the majority of foods from the carbohydrate group and then the amount of protein on your plate naturally will be less.
* When you shop, use the periphery of the grocery store for most of your food choices where you will most often find fruits and vegetables and grains, all great sources of complex carbohydrates and fiber.
* Look for foods that have the vibrant colors — reds, yellows, greens, oranges — which are so great for your health.
* To determine the carbohydrates in common foods, be sure to read the food label.

For more information on these and other important nutrition issues: call 1-800-366-1655 or visit www.eatright.org

Lady Baltimore on a Roll
Baltimore, Maryland

*L*earn to recognize fad diets so you can save yourself the money, time, and effort that you must 'pay' for such short term 'gain', not to mention the possible health risks you might encounter. Instead find a registered dietitian who can work with you to design a plan that meets your needs and your desires and whose insights stay with you for a lifetime. Make balanced nutrition and 'reasonable' eating your 'fad' diet!

I'm expecting this to be my very last public demonstration on cake making so I wanted to go with a really refined carbohydrate swan song! This I could not resist . . . it's a perfect example of what the word 'eclectic' was meant to convey. The Lady Baltimore Cake could be one of the very first to go multi-layered, as many as eight! Here I've kept to the basic white-ish sponge by adapting Susan Purdy's Almond Sponge Roll from her excellent book on low fat baking (Let Them Eat Cake). I've traded height for 'Swiss roll' form. The filling is almost classic. The frosting is an extraordinary citrus flavored seven minute notion from 'New Basics" by Rosso and Lukins — you don't need much of it, but boy it's unique. For those of you with a truly sweet tooth, I offer one word of advice — cook this for a crowd and eat only one slice!

Desserts

Graham Kerr's Place

Ingredients:

Cake (Almond Sponge Roll from
  Let Them Eat Cake by Susan Purdy)
1/2 cup sifted cake flour
1/4 cup sifted cornstarch
1 teaspoon baking powder
2 large eggs, separated plus 2 large egg whites
1/4 teaspoon cream of tartar
6 tablespoons + 1/4 cup granulated sugar
1 tablespoon non-aromatic olive oil
1 teaspoon vanilla extract
1 teaspoon almond extract
1/4 cup powdered sugar

Filling
1/4 cup toasted pecans, chopped, divided
1/4 cup Grape Nuts
6 figs cut in thin strips
1/2 cup chopped raisins, chopped
1/2 teaspoon almond extract
2 cups lowfat yogurt cheese (see 'The Basics')

Frosting
(from *The New Basics* by Rosso and Lukins)
1 egg white
1/2 cup sugar
1/8 teaspoon baking powder
1 tablespoon freshly squeezed lemon juice
1 tablespoon freshly squeezed orange juice
1 teaspoon finely grated orange zest

Lady Baltimore on a Roll

1. Preheat the oven to 350°F (180°C). Spray a 10 1/2" x 15 1/2" (26.5 x 39.5 cm) jelly roll pan and line with parchment or waxed paper. Spray the paper and dust lightly with flour. Sift together the flour, cornstarch, and baking powder and set aside.

2. Beat the egg whites until foamy, add the cream of tartar and gradually sprinkle in 6 tablespoons of the sugar while beating until stiff but not dry. Set aside. Without washing the beaters, whip together the egg yolks, oil, vanilla and almond extracts and the remaining 1/4 cup sugar. Beat on high speed for 3 or 4 minutes until the batter forms a ribbon falling back on itself when the beater is lifted.

3. Fold a third of the beaten whites into the batter, then fold in a few tablespoons of the flour mixture. Fold the rest of the whites and flour, alternately, into the batter, 1/3 of each at a time. Keep it smooth, light and airy. Pour into the prepared pan and smooth gently all the way to the edges. Bake 11 to 13 minutes or until the top is golden and it feels springy to the touch.

4. Sift the powdered sugar on a clean tea towel covering a 10" x 15" (25 x 38 cm) rectangle. When the cake is done, set the sugared towel over the cake and invert. Lift off the pan and remove the paper on the bottom of the cake. Trim the edges a little if they are dry or thin. Fold the edge of the towel over one long side of the cake and roll up while still quite hot. Set it edge seam side down to cool.

5. Combine 3 tablespoons of the pecans, Grape Nuts, figs, and raisins with the almond extract in a small bowl. When the cake is cool, unroll and spread with the yogurt cheese, leaving a bare 3" (8 cm) strip on the far edge. Scatter the fruit and nut mix evenly over the yogurt. Roll tightly and set seam side down on a long serving plate. Trim each end.

6. Combine the egg white, sugar, baking powder, orange juice, lemon juice, and orange zest in the top of a double boiler. Set over boiling water and beat constantly with a hand held electric mixer for 7 minutes or until the frosting is satiny and fluffy. Remove from the heat and spread over the rolled cake. Sprinkle the remaining tablespoon of pecans on top. Cut into 12 servings with a wet knife.

Serves 12

Fad Diets

Registered dietitian Edith Hogan came to talk about fad diets, so I busily recreated the Lady Baltimore Cake (a classic early indulgence). Nobody in a fit would ever suggest this cake in the same breath as the word 'diet'! Strangely, it did fit because it had been moderated and not banned. It seems fair to say that diets that condemn some foods and prefer others in isolation instead of broad based variety are fads and should be cautiously examined. Check the nutrition numbers and portion size of this cake and I think you'll see how it can fit a 'non-fad' diet.

What are the 'fads' in current popular diet programs?

* Nearly half of the American adult population is on a diet or is contemplating a diet because they are overweight. About $50 billion dollars is spent each year on diets or diet related programs, plans, and products. These are often gimmicks that don't work.

* So-called 'high protein' diets are in 'fashion' today. High-protein diets profess that eating carbohydrates is bad and stimulates an excess production of insulin. These diets blame insulin for producing fat storage at an alarming rate, which causes high blood pressure, high cholesterol, and lots of other health problems. They also claim protein and fat does not stimulate insulin, and thus can be eaten in unlimited amounts. People think it works because they lose weight, but the end result is generally weight gain beyond where the dieter started in the first place.

Edith Howard Hogan, RD, LD
Spokesperson, American Dietetic Association

How can we evaluate not only the effectiveness for weight loss but also the health safety of these fad diets?

* Steer clear of diets which claim they produce rapid weight loss, melt fat away, don't require exercise, and are 'easy'.

* Avoid diets that require eating unusual food combinations, emphasize one food group to the exclusion of others, recommend eating 'bizarre' quantities of food, or eating only at a special time of the day.

* Be skeptical of claims for magic or miracle weight loss foods and other secrets or 'cures'.

NUTRITIONAL PROFILE COMPARISON

Per serving	Nutrient Rich	Old Style
calories	250	715
fat (g)	5	31
saturated fat (g)	1	4
carbohydrates (g)	46	105
fiber (g)	2	2
sodium (mg)	132	278

* Always avoid information that is not backed by science or is a result of partial scientific testing.

If a person is trying a fad diet, what can we do to turn this into a long-term, positive and permanent change?

* Capitalize on the fact that they have decided to make a change and reinforce that commitment to change.

* Build upon the initial weight loss and the associated positive feelings by designing a balanced and healthful plan that one can follow forever to avoid the health risks.

* Use the Food Guide Pyramid as a visual aid to show that we can move out of the 'compartmentalizing' of food as we create our own plan that will suit our individualized needs.

* Emphasize that moderation (all foods fit), balance, and exercise must be part of the plan.

* Consult with a registered dietitian who will be a thorough and personal guide on this journey to better health.

For additional information on this topic: call 1-800-366-1655 or contact: www.eatright.org and www.wheatfoods.org

$\mathcal{T}$arte Tatin
Montreal, Quebec

$\mathcal{A}$pple pie is so typically North American, yet when it's quite literally turned upside down, it becomes incredibly French. I can't help but capture memories of Paris bakeries with their long crusty baguettes of French bread, the blossoming mounds of brioche and then, glistening with its deep, caramel glaze, the tarte tatin: crust underneath, apples proudly floating on top. It's so easy to step from Paris to Montreal and in a blink, almost everything looks and sounds the same. For a taste of French Montreal . . . please give this a go!

For a reason now lost in antiquity, it was named Tarte Tatin . . . Tarte because the top crust was now underneath . . . Tatin . . . well that we don't know. What is known is that my version made on television broke when inverted, which, I guess makes me clumsier than Tatin.

Desserts

Ingredients:

1/2 recipe Basic Pie Crust
  (see 'The Basics')
4 1/2 Jonagold or other soft cooking
  apples (Courtland, Macintosh, or
  Northern Spy)
1/4 cup water
1/3 cup sugar
1/4 cup butter flavored margarine
1 teaspoon lemon zest

Tarte Tatin

1. Roll out dough for 1 pie crust to a 9" circle. Lay a cloth over it and set aside. Core, peel and halve the apples. Leaving the apples in halves, lay them on a plate the same size as the pan you are going to use and trim the apples to fit together in a circle of 8 halves with 1 in the center. Set aside.

2. Preheat the oven to 425°F (220°C). Combine the water, sugar and margarine in a chef's pan or heavy-bottomed skillet. Bring to a boil on high heat and stir until it turns golden brown. Pull off the heat and lay the apples in the pan round side down. Scatter the lemon zest over the top. Reduce the heat to medium. Place a lid, 1 size smaller than the lip of the pan, right down on top of the apples. Cook, shaking occasionally, 15 minutes or until the apples are tender. Remove from the heat and cool 10 minutes.

3. Fold the rolled out crust in quarters and lay on the top of the apples, unfolding to cover completely. Tuck the edges down around the hot apples and prick the crust a few times with a fork. Bake 20 to 30 minutes or until the crust is golden brown. Set on a rack and cool slightly, 10 minutes. Place a large inverted plate on top of the crust. Hold with a cloth in both hands and smartly turn it upside down (you *can* do it, *really!*). Then cut in wedges and serve with really good coffee.

Special Techniques:

* Cover the cut apples with water mixed with lemon juice to prevent the apples from turning brown.

Serves 8

Listening to Your Heart Doctor

When we invited cardiologist John Schroeder back to The Gathering Place, we asked him if changing our diet — lowering the amount of saturated fats and sodium, for example — and exercising more was enough to prevent heart disease. While in some cases, these changes in lifestyle may be enough, in others there is a need for medication. Consulting with a doctor concerning something as 'absolutely' vital as your heart is a sign of courage, not cowardice — and following good medical advice is a sign of wisdom.

Why is heart medication sometimes necessary?

In most cases, the diagnosis of high blood pressure and elevated cholesterol makes it imperative to receive medication in order to reduce risk of further disease and prevent serious health complications, including heart attack or stroke. We need to understand the need for medication in addition to lifestyle changes.

What medications are commonly prescribed for treating heart disease?

* Statin drugs which lower cholesterol levels.
* Blood pressure medicines which lower blood pressure.
* Aspirin (baby) which 'thin' the blood without affecting the stomach adversely.
* Vitamin E (400 IU) and Vitamin C (500 mg) which may have beneficial anti-oxidant effects.

Some people neglect to take their medication, however. Remember, if you don't take the medication prescribed, the likelihood of experiencing a heart attack or stroke is much greater!

Why don't some people follow the medication regime doctor's prescribe?

* Heart disease and high blood pressure are generally asymptomatic, so you don't feel anything until there is a problem.
* Side effects.
* The 'it-won't-happen-to-me' syndrome.
* Cost.

John Schroeder, MD
Professor, Cardiovascular Medicine,
Stanford University
Co-Author, *The Stanford University Healthy Heart Cookbook & Life Plan*

NUTRITIONAL PROFILE COMPARISON

Per serving	Nutrient Rich	Old Style
calories	250	715
fat (g)	5	31
saturated fat (g)	1	4
carbohydrates (g)	46	105
fiber (g)	2	2
sodium (mg)	132	278

What else can you advise?

* Keep in mind that you are not a failure if you need to take medication in order to be healthy. In many instances changing lifestyle factors may not be enough and medication may help to decrease your risk.

* If your physician prescribes medicine, take it in order to be well.

* Communicate with your physician. Discuss your needs and problems. Let you doctor know if your medication does not seem to be agreeing with you. There are probably others that would work just as well and suit your body better, but you might never know until you ask!

* And put medication in a place where you remember to take it — for example, with your toothbrush.

For further information on this topic contact: http://cvmed.stanford.edu/default.htm
Or http://www.stanfordlifeplan.com/

Blackberry Warm Egg Custard

Toronto, Ontario

Everything I read and instinctively feel is true makes me believe that eating organic food, grown naturally and freshly prepared, without biotechnological intervention and chemical processing, is the best way. But can we feed the world this way? Research indicates that by 2050 we will need to triple global food production to feed the planet. Can this be done organically? Current advances in food technology, tempered with time-honored organic wisdom, may hold the promise of feeding the hungry with healthy food today and in the future.

The Italian people have a delicious dessert called Zabaglione, a frothy egg yolk custard liberally laced with a sweet dessert wine. This recipe is almost like an early chemistry experiment. When the thickened 'wine' is added to the beaten eggs, an unusual frothy cream expansion takes place. To my taste, it is far better to serve it warm. By no means is this classic a major threat to heart health — I simply wanted to bring it home for those of us who don't have a taste for alcohol. This one is, believe it or not, 'no' fat!

Desserts

Ingredients:

1 pound fresh or frozen and
  thawed blackberries
1 1/2 cups de-alcoholized fruity white wine
3 tablespoons real maple syrup
1/4 teaspoon almond extract
1/4 teaspoon vanilla extract
2 tablespoons cornstarch mixed with
  1/4 cup de-alcoholized fruity white wine
1/4 cup sugar
1 cup egg substitute

Blackberry Warm Egg Custard

1. Divide 1 1/4 cups of the blackberries among 8 wine glasses (10 ounce, 28 g). Press the rest of the blackberries through a sieve. Discard the seeds and set the juice aside.

2. Bring the wine to a boil in a medium saucepan. Add the maple syrup, almond and vanilla extracts. Stir in the slurry, bring back to a boil, and stir 30 seconds while it thickens. Set aside to cool slightly.

3. Heat a small amount of water in a medium saucepan. Set a round copper or other metal bowl on top to create a double boiler. Reduce the heat to a simmer. Pour the sugar and egg substitute into the bowl and beat over the simmering water until frothy, thick, creamy, and more than tripled in volume, 3 minutes.

4. Pour the wine syrup into the egg mixture in a thin stream, whisking all the time. Add 3/4 of the blackberry puree, mixing well. Spoon the pudding over the blackberries in the glasses. Swirl the remaining puree on top of each dessert.

Serves 8

Global Food Issues

When Dennis Avery, Director of the Center for Global Food Issues at the Hudson Institute and author of Saving the World with Plastics and Pesticides, appeared on The Gathering Place, his views on managing our food supply initially 'brushed my fur the wrong way'. While I was prepared to counter his belief in technology with my organic articles of faith, I found myself moderating my absolutes when I discovered he had been raised on a farm — and as we discussed the very real problem of how to feed the hungry. Perhaps we can find a way for the organic and the technological ways to meet, reasonably, in service of the optimum health of everyone on our planet.

What is the Hudson Institute?

The Hudson Institute is a 'think tank' where we look as far into the future as we think it is to rational to look and think about how good technology can help us to solve the problems that seem to be out there.

What 'food' problems do you foresee?

While we live in a society that has the safest, most abundant food supply that humanity has ever seen because of pasteurization, fortified flour, and access to low-cost fresh and preserved fruits and vegetables, food yields are low, which can endanger not only future generations of humans but also wildlife. We obviously need to increase agricultural yields.

Consider these future facts:

* We now use 37% of the earth's land area for farming and cannot feed everyone adequately. By 2050 we will need three times the amount of food, not only because our world population is growing but also because we will consume more food as the world becomes more affluent. Where will we find the land to grow the food without infringing upon wildlife preserves and forests?
* Chemical fertilizers, pesticides, and biotechnology have been beneficial in increasing yields on existing farm land. We have saved land and therefore saved wildlife. Should we not continue to pursue this avenue for managing our food supply?

Dennis Avery, MS
Director, Center for Global Food Issues,
The Hudson Institute
Author, Saving the World with Plastics and Pesticides

NUTRITIONAL PROFILE COMPARISON

Per serving	Nutrient Rich	Old Style
calories	124	132
fat (g)	0	4
saturated fat (g)	0	1
carbohydrates (g)	27	18
fiber (g)	3	3
sodium (mg)	55	86

* While agricultural technology and food processing food are sometimes attacked for polluting the land and exposing us to chemical risks, consider the bacterial risk of organically grown foods in previous generations that were not processed or preserved. Should we abandon one potential risk in favor of another? Can we not find a way to employ the best of both agricultural and food management practices?

For further information on this topic contact: www.hudson.org/cgfi

ummer Pudding
Victoria, British Columbia

*E*ating and sleeping — we don't seem to have the time these days to do either one well. But cheating on 'sleep' is no less dangerous than cheating on food. Just as our diet is sometimes nutritionally deficient, so we are often sleep starved or deprived. We need to sleep well to be well. Try sleeping a bit longer each night so you have more time to dream of good food!

The Pacific Northwest of the United States and Canada is one of the most prolific berry growing areas in the world. It has also attracted immigrants from the Northern European nations. Many from the British Isles came to settle on Vancouver Island in and around the city of Victoria. Oak Bay borders Victoria and seems, at times, to be more English than England! Especially The Blethering Place, a tearoom that gained its title from the verb 'to blether', meaning, 'to speak lots of largely unrelated words'. Actually, I've had some really meaningful discussions over a pot of tea (complete with knitted cosy!) and a piece of Bumbleberry Pie in this very hospitable restaurant. This time, we wanted to introduce you to the Summer Pudding, a wonderful triumph of summer berries that can also be made from frozen berries when the season comes to its inevitable rainy conclusion.

Desserts

Ingredients:

1 1/2 cups fresh or frozen
   unsweetened raspberries
1 1/2 cups fresh or frozen
   unsweetened blackberries
1 1/2 cups fresh or frozen unsweetened
   strawberries, sliced
1 1/2 cups fresh or frozen blueberries
1/2 cup sugar
1 packet unflavored gelatin
3 tablespoons cold water
3 tablespoons boiling water
14 Italian lady fingers (savoiardi)

Garnish
1 cup vanilla yogurt cheese (see 'The Basics')
8 sprigs fresh mint

Summer Pudding

1. Combine the berries in a large saucepan, add the sugar and bring just to a boil to break out the juice and dissolve the sugar. Set aside to cool. Sprinkle the gelatin over the cold water in a small bowl to soften for a few minutes. Add the boiling water to completely dissolve the gelatin. Stir into the berries.

2. Line a 6 cup bowl with the ladyfingers. Cut 2 to fit the bottom. Pour the berries into the mold and trim the cookies to the top of the berry mixture. Set a small plate on top and weight it with 3 full cans. Let it set in the refrigerator for at least 3 hours or, better yet, overnight so the juice will fully penetrate the cookies.

3. Set the mold in a larger bowl of warm water to loosen and turn out onto a plate. Cut into 8 wedges and serve with a dollop of vanilla yogurt cheese and a sprig of mint.

Serves 8

Special Techniques:

* A vegetarian substitute for gelatin is Agar Agar (seaweed derivative).
* Avoid cloudy gelatin dishes: Start with 3 tablespoons of cold water, sprinkle 1 tablespoon of gelatin on top, and let it set for a few minutes. Add three tablespoons of hot water, which will dissolve the gelatin perfectly.

Power Sleep

Professor James B. Mass, author of Power Sleep, came by The Gathering Place to discuss the health dangers of sleep deprivation and the benefits of a good night's rest — and believe me, what he said didn't put us to sleep! While I had always thought that seven hours of sleep was really enough, Dr Maas recommended nine hours. What an incredible difference it's made. Treena and I are now seldom tired during the day. We fall asleep easily and awaken eagerly. Both of us are indebted to Dr Maas for our new lease on life (literally!)

How do we know if we are sleep deprived?

If you need an alarm clock to wake up, you are sleep deprived. If you fall asleep instantly, you are sleep starved.

What happens when we are sleep deprived?

* Even minimal loss of sleep over time makes us feel 'stupid', seriously affecting our concentration and reaction time.
* Studies where participants were limited to 4 hours of sleep for 6 nights showed that blood sugar (cortisol activity) and the sympathetic nervous system increased dramatically.
* Study participants were actually aging overnight, leading to early onset of type II diabetes, obesity, and hypertension.

How do we figure out how much sleep we need?

Keep track of how many hours you are sleeping a night and how alert you are during the day, recognizing that most of us have a mid-day dip. Add 15 minutes increments of sleep to the length of time you have been sleeping for a week until you are alert all day long. Most people need to add at least one more hour of sleep to their current sleep habits. For those of us who sleep 8 hours already, alertness can increase by 25% when you add an hour of sleep.

What do you recommend for getting a 'good night's sleep'?

* Set the 'stage' for the 'theater of the night'. Make sure the bedroom is quite dark and cool, about 65°F. Make sure you have a good pillow (pillow test: fold the pillow in half, if it springs forward by itself it is fine, if not, get a new one). Make sure you have a great

James B. Maas, PhD
Professor, Psychology, Cornell University
Author, *Power Sleep*

NUTRITIONAL PROFILE COMPARISON

Per serving	Nutrient Rich	Old Style
calories	208	464
fat (g)	2	15
saturated fat (g)	5	8
carbohydrates (g)	45	80
fiber (g)	4	8
sodium (mg)	83	202

When we move people from 7 to 8 hours of sleep, they all say after 12 weeks of going to bed earlier, they never knew what it was like to be awake!

mattress with pocketed coil spring technology so all coils are separately based. Set aside a worry time to write down or tape record your worries to get them off your mind. Read for relaxation before you fall asleep. Take a warm bath.

* Don't sleep in on the weekends. This will mess up your schedule. You have to be regular to get the best sleep, so go to bed at the same time every day of the week. A normal, well-rested person takes 15 minutes to 20 minutes to fall asleep

Television and clocks with red LED displays will probably disturb your sleep, so turn them off before you fall asleep.

How about 'power' naps?

Thirty-eight percent of the workforce naps on the job every week, usually in the parking lot or bathroom stall. Find a better place where you can put your head down for 15-20 minutes, but never 'power' nap for more than 20 minutes or you will feel even more tired.

How can we avoid 'jet lag'?

* Set your clock to the destination time and start living on that schedule before you fly.
* Avoid alcohol and heavy meals on the plane.
* Going Eastbound: if you land early, get out in the daylight and reset your clocks.
* Going Westbound: stay up later in the day.
* Don't take a power nap when you arrive — that will keep you on your local time.

For more information on this topic or to be in touch with our guest contact: www.Powersleep.com

Indian Pudding
New Hampshire

Gold and silver are not the most valuable minerals in the world. Potassium, magnesium, and calcium are essential for maintaining good health, but our diet is often deficient in these trace minerals. Make your diet 'rich' by eating more bananas and melons, beans and lentils, and low fat dairy products, which are high in potassium, calcium, and magnesium. Mineral wealth and good health are synonymous, in this case.

The term 'Indian Pudding' would certainly lead one to believe that it existed prior to the earliest settlers. Surprisingly, this wasn't so. It was simply the use of corn that gave rise to the name. To trace its roots back to England's 'Hasty Pudding' could easily be seen as an 'un-American' activity, so I'll resist! This is my take on a new regional dish with maple syrup, cranberries, and hazelnuts. The seasoning use of cinnamon and ginger will have to be taken with a pinch of salt . . . I've yet to find either growing naturally in the Northeast!

Desserts

Ingredients:

2 teaspoons molasses
1/4 cup whole hazelnuts, divided
2 1/2 cups 1% milk
5 tablespoons yellow cornmeal
pinch salt
scant 1/2 teaspoon cinnamon
scant 1/2 teaspoon ginger
1/4 cup maple syrup
1/4 cup + 2 tablespoons dried cranberries,
 divided
1/2 cup dried apples, roughly chopped
1/2 cup egg substitute
1 tablespoon arrowroot

Sauce
1 cup nonfat yogurt cheese (see 'The Basics')
2 tablespoons maple syrup
1/8 teaspoon cinnamon
1/8 teaspoon ginger

Indian Pudding

1. Preheat the oven to 350°F (180°C). Grease a 6 cup loaf pan with pan spray. Spoon the molasses into the bottom of the pan and set aside. Roast the hazelnuts in a small metal pan for 5 minutes in the preheated oven. Rub the hot roasted nuts in a kitchen towel to remove some of the skins. Chop roughly and set aside. Reduce the oven heat to 300°F (150°C).

2. Heat the milk in a large saucepan on medium high until bubbles appear around the edge. Whisk in the cornmeal and cook until the mixture boils, then remove from the heat. Add the salt, cinnamon, ginger, maple syrup, 2 tablespoons of the nuts, 1/4 cup of the cranberries, and the apple pieces. Combine the egg substitute and arrowroot and stir into the milk mixture.

3. Pour into the prepared loaf pan. Set into a larger pan and put in the oven. Pour hot water into the larger pan until the water comes about half way up the pudding pan to make a water bath. Lay a piece of oiled foil over the top and bake 2 hours.

4. Make the sauce by combing the yogurt cheese, maple syrup, cinnamon and ginger. Refrigerate until ready to serve. When the pudding is done, cool on a rack. Tip out of the pan and cut in 8 slices. Serve with a dollop of the sauce and a sprinkle of the reserved nuts and cranberries.

Serves 8

Special Techniques:

* Roasting Nuts: roast nuts when using them in a dish to accentuate the flavor and bring out the natural oils for a greater depth of flavor.
* Bain Marie: water is placed in a larger pan so that the loaf pan containing the ingredients can cook evenly without scorching.

Biotechnology

Registered dietitian Felicia Busch came by The Gathering Place to explore the potential benefits and risks of foods grown with biotechnology properties. Biotech foods are just as nutritious and in the future they may be even more nutritious due to biotechnology enhancements. Feeding the world adequately, safely, and nutritiously is certainly something we aspire to do.

What is food biotechnology?

* Biotechnology is the next step beyond the cross-breeding of plants. Through cross-breeding you take the best of both plants, mix them together and hope you get the best traits. What biotechnology does is simplify this process, so you take one trait out of a plant, put it into another plant and then you do not have to mess around with years and years of trying to get the traits together. It is simply an enhancement of cross-breeding.

* The United States Food and Drug Administration states that if you change a plant that is not nearly identical to the plant you started with, you must label it as a product of biotechnology, but the products on the market today are substantially equivalent so they do not need a label. In the grocery store today, 25-75% of all corn, soybean, and potato products are biotech, but they are not labeled as such because they are not substantially different.

What are the benefits of biotechnology?

Environmentally, we are able to reduce pesticides and chemicals, which is good for the farmer and the consumer. With 'no-till' technology, we won't loose as much topsoil before the seed is planted.

How safe is biotechnology?

* We have been practicing biotechnology since 1800 BC, when we first learned how to ferment grapes into wine (using an organism to change this food into something else) and through the cheese-making process where instead of using rennet we use an enzyme that has been developed through the use of biotechnology called chymesin

Felicia Busch, MPH, RD, FADA
Spokesperson, American Dietetic Association

NUTRITIONAL PROFILE COMPARISON

Per serving	Nutrient Rich	Old Style
calories	209	319
fat (g)	5	19
saturated fat (g)	1	11
carbohydrates (g)	33	34
fiber (g)	2	1
sodium (mg)	114	271

(half of all the cheese we buy has been produced through biotechnology). It has been tested more than the traditional foods that we eat through cross-breading.

* There is one area of caution to be found in the testing: allergens. People with food allergies — to peanuts, for example — might be affected by biotechnology foods with these allergenic elements. Accordingly, researchers are careful to avoid foods with allergenic properties.

Is *biotechnology less expensive?*

The seed is more costly but the farmer does not have to pay for all the chemicals and pesticides, so in the long run it could be more cost effective.

Is *it better for you?*

Biotechnology may be beneficial for third world countries that have only one crop they rely on because technology may make the crop drought and pest resistant, making it possible to avoid famine and plague. For some populations, like the Chinese who may be allergic to the staple food of rice, biotechnology can take the allergen out of rice.

For further information on this topic contact: www.ificinfo.health.org/index14.htm

*A*isle Cake
Chattanooga, Tennessee

*C*offee is one of those foods like chocolate that we are tempted to overdo, but like all other foods, coffee can be enjoyed 'within reason' — without adversely affecting our health and without disturbing our sleep. Consumed moderately, coffee may even be more enjoyable!

Years and years ago, good friends asked if I would make them a wedding cake. I agreed and for the first time in the world (to my certain knowledge) an 'aisle' cake was born. Recently, I did my seventh Aisle for our youngest daughter Kareena and her now new husband Michael in Chattanooga, Tennessee. Basically, it's a well-made sponge cake. Susan Purdy makes a great orange cake that uses only one large egg (and three whites). This is cut to make a cake four inches wide and about one inch for every person attending the ceremony. My largest is now 485 inches long! The bride and groom stand either side of the long table and greet everyone, cutting the cake and serving both sides. I've taken the cake idea and down-scaled it for a party at home. While a wedding cake had to have a butter-cream icing, it's possible for a party to use a radical frosting made with yogurt. It works very well indeed, with only 4% of its calories from saturated fat. Oh yes . . . your guests will ask for more!

Desserts

Ingredients:

Orange Loaf Cake (adapted from Susan
  Purdy's *Let Them Eat Cake*)
2 1/4 cups sifted cake flour
  (you must sift the flour before measuring,
  for it will make a large difference in the
  total volume of the flour used)
1 teaspoon baking powder
1/4 teaspoon baking soda
1/2 teaspoon salt
3 large egg whites, at room temperature
1 1/4 cups granulated sugar, divided
1/3 cup non-aromatic olive oil
1 large egg
1/3 cup plain, nonfat yogurt
1/3 cup applesauce
2 teaspoons vanilla extract
1 teaspoon orange extract
grated zest from 2 oranges (2 tablespoons)
1/2 cup fresh orange juice

Frosting
9 tablespoons nonfat dried milk powder
1/2 cup ice water
3 tablespoons superfine sugar
1 teaspoon non-aromatic olive oil
1/4 teaspoon vanilla
1 packet unflavored gelatin
3 tablespoons cold water
3 tablespoons boiling water
1 cup yogurt cheese (see 'The Basics')
1 cup sliced strawberries
2 kiwis, peeled and sliced

Aisle Cake

1. Preheat the oven to 350°F (180°C) with the rack in the center of the oven. Coat 2 medium loaf pans with pan spray then dust with flour. Place a mixing bowl and beater in the freezer to chill for the frosting. Combine the cake flour, baking powder, soda, and salt in a medium bowl with a whisk.

2. Whip the egg whites until foamy, gradually add 1/4 cup of the sugar and continue beating until stiff peaks form.

3. In a separate bowl beat the oil, the remaining cup of sugar, whole egg, yogurt, applesauce, vanilla and orange extracts, orange zest and orange juice together until combined. Beat in the flour mixture in small amounts. Fold in the beaten whites.

4. Divide between the 2 prepared pans and bake in the preheated oven 35 minutes or until golden brown and springy to the touch. There will be a small crack down the center of the cake and a toothpick inserted in the center will come out clean. Cool in the pans for 10 minutes before removing to a rack to cool completely. Cut the cakes in half horizontally. Cut a 1/2" x 2" (1.5 x 5 cm) ditch lengthwise down the center of each half; this will hold the fruit in place. Set aside while you make the frosting.

5. To make the frosting: beat the dried milk and ice water together in the chilled mixing bowl with the chilled beater for a full 6 minutes. Gradually beat in the sugar, then the oil and vanilla. Sprinkle the gelatin over the cold water in a small bowl to soften for 1 minute. Stir in the boiling water to dissolve completely. Combine the beaten milk with the dissolved gelatin and yogurt cheese.

6. Cut 2 pieces of cardboard just a little shorter than the cake in length and a little wider on each side. Cover with waxed paper or foil. Set a cake half on each piece of cardboard. Spoon some of the frosting into the ditch of one half of each cake. Arrange the strawberries and kiwi slices down the center on top of the filling. Spoon more filling on the fruit and place the other half of the cake on the top. Push the 2 cakes together and cover with the rest of the frosting. Garnish with extra strawberries and kiwi slices and refrigerate until you are ready to cut it. You can make just 1 finished cake by halving the frosting recipe and freezing the second cake.

Serves 16

Counting Caffeine

When Stephen Cherniske agreed to appear on *The Gathering Place*, we knew we would have to brew a 'healthy' cup of coffee for the author of **Caffeine Blues**! You do not have to eliminate this drink totally from your diet but your health may improve if you decrease your consumption. Just get a better grip of how much you are consuming now and see if you can't keep it within reason. Moderation is the key!

Stephen Cherniske, MS
Author, *Caffeine Blues*

What is a moderate amount of caffeine to consume in a day?

* A moderate intake of caffeine is 200-300 milligrams each day. The following beverages contain, on average, the listed amount of caffeine. However, various brands and the method of preparation may alter the amount slightly.

Brewed Coffee (6oz.)	103 mg
Instant Coffee (6 oz.)	57 mg
Brewed Tea (6 oz.)	36 mg
Instant Tea (8 oz.)	30 mg
Cola-type Soda (12 oz.)	46 mg

But beware, coffee cups are growing. Most people start out with a 6 oz. cup, followed by a 14 oz. mug, and often upgrade to a 24 oz. coffee tumbler, or a 34 oz. jug which may yield 800 or 900 mg of caffeine — even a specially designed commuter mug which could contain up to 1200 mg of caffeine.

Also, be aware that some medications also contain a fair amount of caffeine. Check with your physician if you are concerned about the amount of caffeine your medication contains.

Anacin	32 mg
Dexatrim	200mg
Excedrin	65mg
Midol	32mg
No-Doz	100mg
Vivarin	200mg

NUTRITIONAL PROFILE COMPARISON

Per serving	Nutrient Rich	Old Style
calories	221	714
fat (g)	5	49
saturated fat (g)	1	29
carbohydrates (g)	38	64
fiber (g)	1	1
sodium (mg)	172	273

What are the health risks in consuming too much caffeine?

There is a concern that caffeine may be addictive and that some people may become tolerant at very large doses. If you have headaches or feel a low when you don't have your morning cup of coffee, try to wean yourself down and see if you feel any better. Headache and depression may drive people back to the caffeine. If you feel any of these symptoms of excess caffeine, see for yourself how much you consume in a day. Keep a record of your coffee, tea, and soda intake and add up your daily total. If you consume over 200-300 milligrams a day, consider replacing some of your caffeinated beverages with decaffeinated varieties.

Can we substitute another beverage or food for a caffeine-laden one?

When trying a new food or beverage in an effort to replace an old one (like an herbal coffee to replace regular coffee), try the following techniques:

* Follow the same ritual for preparation for the new as you did for the old.
* Try three times and on the third day you may even like it much better.
* Never expect it to taste the same as the food or beverage you are trying to replace. Recognize that it will be different and try to like it for what it is instead of what it is not.

For more information on this topic: contact www.oasisnetwork.com or www.ificinfo. health.org/brochure/caffeine.htm. Note: These two websites provide two different perspectives. If you still have questions, check with your physician who can help to make a personalized recommendation for you.

Key Lime Pie
Miami, Florida

Our children are flunking 'eating'! According to a United States government research study, only one percent of children have eating patterns consistent with dietary recommendations. Unhealthy eating and inactivity are the root causes of overweight and obesity, and the percentage of young people who are overweight has more than doubled in the past 30 years. It's time to help our children improve their 'nutrition' grades.

The chances are that you may have never tasted the classic version of this famous regional dish. It comes from the extreme south of Florida where, years ago, dairy cattle were few and evaporated milk was the norm. It was also before graham crackers (really there was such a time!), so the crust was pastry. The eggs clabbered with the lime (citrus awranti floia) and evaporated milk set up well. There was no cream, so the meringue uses the egg whites. As for the bright green color you see today? — you might as well forget it. No lime I've ever seen produces that color — so it is artificial, OK?

Desserts

Ingredients:

1/2 recipe Basic Pie Crust (see 'The Basics')

Filling
4 teaspoons lime zest
1/2 cup freshly squeezed lime juice
4 egg yolks
1 14-ounce can nonfat sweetened
   condensed milk

Meringue
2 egg whites
1/4 teaspoon cream of tartar
1/4 cup granulated sugar
1/4 teaspoon vanilla

Key Lime Pie

1. Preheat the oven to 425°F (220°C). Roll out the pie crust to fit an 8" pie tin. Lay the rolled dough in the pan without stretching it and crimp the edge. Prick with a fork. Lay a piece of parchment or waxed paper in the pie shell and pour in enough beans to cover the bottom. These will act as pie weights to keep it from bubbling up while baking. Bake for 8 minutes or until golden brown.

2. Reduce the heat to 350°F (180°C). Combine the lime zest, juice, egg yolks and milk in a bowl with a whisk. Pour into the baked shell and bake 15 minutes. When the pie is done, raise the oven temperature back to 425°F (220°C).

3. While the pie is baking, make the meringue. Beat the eggs until foamy. Then add the cream of tartar. When they reach soft peaks, sprinkle in the sugar and continue to beat until the meringue holds stiff peaks. Beat the vanilla in at the end. Spoon the meringue around the sides of the pie and seal to prevent it from shrinking. Scoop the rest into the center and smooth it all. Pick up peaks with the back of a spoon and bake for 4 minutes or until golden brown.

Serves 8

School Food Programs

Good food for our children — this is a recipe we must work on together, at home and at school, morning, noon, and night. We urge you to get involved on every level. Students should have choices — fruit at sporting events, 100% juice in vending machines — just imagine the possibilities! School meal programs can be part of the solution, but good nutrition must start at home. Children's brains and bodies need calories and nutrients to function at optimal levels. Parents and concerned citizens can all get involved to make a difference in the lives of the young ones we love, those who will someday be our future.

What is the current nutritional status of children in the United States?

* 45% of elementary children eat less than one serving of fruit a day.

* 20% eat less than one serving of vegetables a day.

* More than half do not eat the recommended servings of grains.

* Only 18% of girls ages 9-19 meet their calcium requirement.

* About two-thirds eat more fat than is recommended.

Martha Conklin, PhD, RD
Director, National Food Service
Management Institute,
Applied Research Division,
University of Southern Mississippi
Co-Author, *Managing Child Nutrition Programs*

How can school food programs help to solve this serious health problem?

* Research has shown that children who eat from the School Lunch programs consume more milk, fruits, and vegetables than children who bring their lunches from home.

* Research also indicates students in breakfast programs have improved scores on academic tests and absenteeism has decreased, along with trips to the school nurse and restless/acting out behaviors in the classroom.

What are the nutritional guidelines for school food programs in the United States?

* Lunch meals that receive reimbursement from the USDA must deliver 1/3 the RDA for calories and nutrients. The levels are graduated, based on children's ages.

* Weekly meals programs must meet the nutritional goals associated with the U.S. Dietary Guidelines for Americans: no more than 30% of the calories, averaged over a week's menus, can be derived from fat, and less than 10% of these calories should be

NUTRITIONAL PROFILE COMPARISON

Per serving	Nutrient Rich	Old Style
calories	249	437
fat (g)	7	24
saturated fat (g)	2	14
fiber (g)	0	1
sodium (mg)	131	201

derived from saturated fat. Goals also include increasing fiber and decreasing the intake of simple sugars and salt.

What can we do to help?

* Encourage 'nutrition' education as part of a coordinated school health curriculum.

* Make sure physical education is provided in schools.

* Make sure school food service meals meet the USDA nutrition standards.

* If a la carte items on the cafeteria line, vending machines, snack bars and school stores are available, be sure they contain healthy choices.

* Make sure the school schedules meals when children are hungry — not at 10 a.m. or 2 p.m. — and provides adequate time for children to enjoy their meals with friends.

* Aim to involve students and parents in establishing food and nutrition policies for the entire school district.

For more information on this topic, contact: American School Food Service Association at www.asfsa.org. For more information on our guest or to order a copy of the book *Managing Child Nutrition Programs: Leadership for Excellence* by J. Martin and M.T. Conklin contact: www.aspenpublishers.com.

# Sweet Potato Pie
Atlanta, Georgia

ome recipes say it all when you read the title and see the pictures. Sweet potato pie is perhaps the best example in this book. Don't you get a twinge of promised satisfaction and comfort just looking at the words and images? But the challenge remains to make these special comfort foods a little less 'risky' but no less satisfying. Now it's up to you to see if I did so — in this recipe and in the others featured on The Gathering Place!

If you love to have a piece of pie, even if, like Treena and I, you call for one portion, two long spoons and a whistle (we think this is funny . . . please write if it isn't clear!). Anyway . . . if you truly crave pie, why not try one with our special crust and filled with anti-oxidants . . . oh how sweet it is! This is a lovely rendition of deep southern comfort food with the unusual sparkle of a molasses spiked yogurt cheese topping. Oh, by the way, I've managed to remove over 200 calories and 20 grams of fat! If you use two long spoons, the aerobic exercise may even deal with a few of those left behind!

Ingredients:

1/2 Basic Pie Crust Recipe (see 'The Basics')

Filling
2 cups mashed sweet potatoes
1 tablespoon butter flavored margarine
1/2 cup egg substitute
1/4 cup firmly packed brown sugar
1 tablespoon molasses
3/4 cup low fat evaporated milk
1/4 teaspoon ground nutmeg
1/4 teaspoon ground cinnamon
1/4 teaspoon ground ginger

Topping
1 tablespoon maple syrup
1 1/2 cup low fat yogurt cheese
 (see 'The Basics')

Sweet Potato Pie

1. Preheat the oven to 425°F (220°C). Roll out the pie crust to fit a 9" pie tin. Lay the rolled dough in the pan without stretching it and crimp the edge. Prick with a fork. Lay a piece of parchment or waxed paper in the pie shell and pour in enough beans to cover the bottom. These will act as pie weights to keep it from bubbling up while baking. Bake for 8 minutes or until golden brown. Reduce the heat to 350°F (180°C).

2. Combine the mashed sweet potatoes, margarine, egg substitute, brown sugar, molasses, milk, nutmeg, cinnamon, and ginger. Pour into the baked crust and smooth. Cover the rim of the pie crust with strips of aluminum foil. Bake 45 to 55 minutes or until a knife inserted in the center comes out clean. Cool slightly before serving.

3. Stir the maple syrup into the yogurt cheese and refrigerate until ready to use. Cut the pie into 8 pieces and serve with a dollop of yogurt topping.

Serves 8

Food for the Needy

Here is another 'seventh guest' plan for sharing our food wealth with others to ensure their good health, but on a big scale. Former Undersecretary of Farm and Foreign Agricultural Services, August Schumacher, joined us on The Gathering Place to describe the 'WIC' and 'Farmers' Markets Coupons' programs sponsored by the government of the United States for ensuring all citizens have access to fresh fruit and vegetables for their diet.

How is the United States government working to get fruits and vegetables to those in need?

* WIC : The Women, Infant and Children (WIC) program is aimed at producing food security for those who may be left out. The focus is on supplying orange juice, formula, milk, cheese, and other juices to those in need.

* Farmer's Market Coupons: Coupons are provided to those in need to purchase fruits and vegetables, which not only helps them but also the local farmer. Forty states, 10,000 small farmers, and 1.5 million women and children are participating in this program.

August Schumacher
Former USDA Undersecretary of Farm and Foreign Agricultural Services

How do people get the Farmer's Market coupons?

* Coupons are available through the Women, Infant and Children Program for young mothers and single parents who have limited income. Coupons are distributed monthly.

How effective are these programs?

* Research shows that people participating in this program consume 25% more fruits and vegetables, so it is a 'jump-start' for these women and children.

* People using the coupons have interchange with the farmer and better understand the process of how fruits and vegetables go from the farm to the table.

* Farmers are pleased with success of the program — their income goes up 30%-40% in some cases — and they love to see the children coming into their markets.

NUTRITIONAL PROFILE COMPARISON

Per serving	Nutrient Rich	Old Style
calories	282	501
fat (g)	9	29
saturated fat (g)	2	14
carbohydrates (g)	43	56
fiber (g)	2	2
sodium (mg)	158	357

* Farmers' Markets have increased in number from 1,000 to 3,000, especially in the inner-city where there is a great need to serve the low-income population.

For further information on this topic contact: www.ams.usda.gov/farmersmarkets or www.fns.usda.gov/wicfarmersmarkets

*A*pple and Pear Crisp

Hyde Park, New York

A final word from the excellent book, Techniques of Healthy Cooking, *by the Culinary Institute of America — 'Good nutrition is nothing more than good food, properly selected and carefully prepared. And nothing less.'*

Throughout our travels in the United States, we asked the very well-equipped researchers at the Culinary Institute of America to help us track down the real comfort foods that so many of us enjoy. In the midst of the list, came the fruit cobbler or crisp or crumble and, wonder of wonders, it was the dish we decided to do at the Culinary Institute itself in Hyde Park, New York, near Poughkeepsie. The recipe took on a couple of innovative twists and turns out to be a real winner. I might add (for the record) how much I enjoy being a visiting professor of this great culinary school!

Ingredients.

Fruit

3 cooking apples (Jonagold, Winesap,
   Northern Spy, or other tart flavorful apple)
3 Bosc pears
1/2 cup golden raisins
2 cups de-alcoholized fruity white wine
   (I like Ariel blanc)
1/8 teaspoon ground cloves

Topping

1/2 cup old-fashioned oats
3 tablespoons sliced almonds
1/2 cup low fat graham crackers crumbs
1/2 cup brown sugar
1 teaspoon cinnamon
1/4 teaspoon nutmeg
3 tablespoons butter flavored stick
   margarine

Sauce

1/2 cup low fat vanilla yogurt

Apple and Pear Crisp

1. Preheat the oven to 350°F (180°C). Peel and core the apples and cut into eighths. Peel and core the pears and cut into quarters. Place in a large skillet, add the raisins, wine and cloves, and cover with a piece of waxed paper cut to fit. Bring to a boil, lower the heat and poach gently 15 minutes or until tender but not mushy. Drain, reserving the liquid, and lay the fruit in an 8"x 8" (20 x 20 cm) baking dish.

2. Combine the oats, almonds, graham cracker crumbs, sugar, cinnamon, and nutmeg in a bowl. Stir in the margarine until the mixture holds together in a crumble. Scatter over the fruit and bake, uncovered, in the preheated oven 30 minutes or until golden and crisp on top.

3. Pour the reserved liquid back into the skillet and boil vigorously until reduced to about 2 tablespoons. Take off the heat and stir in the yogurt. Cut the crisp into 9 pieces and serve with the yogurt sauce.

Serves 9

The Future of Food

"*Healthy food starts with a respect for food,*" Ferdinand Metz, President of the Culinary Institute of America, explained when he visited The Gathering Place. '*And to have respect for food you have to appreciate it and possibly have been without it at one time or another. The evolution of healthy foods is an outgrowth of hard work and deep thinking at the CIA.*" There is nothing covert about this 'CIA'!

What is the Culinary Institute of America?

The CIA is a school where 2200 students are being educated in the culinary arts on two campuses (Hyde Park, New York, and Napa, California). We graduate about 1300 chefs annually. In addition, over 10,000 professionals each year come to one of the two campuses for continuing education, which creates a great synergy of minds, because these are the people who often employ the students.

Ferdinand Metz, CMC, MBA
President, The Culinary Institute of America

What are the challenges today's chefs face? What are their goals?

* Creating a healthy cuisine but *not* at the expense of having it flavorless. When fat is reduced in food, you have to become a better cook. At St. Andrew Café on the CIA campus, the kitchen is different from most because there is no steam table or deep fryer; the staff wanted to make a statement in order to show the students that you can cook wonderful food without these standard pieces of equipment that often affect the flavor and healthful qualities of food. Grilling and poaching are great methods of cooking where the aromas and flavors are accentuated.

* Cooking with less fat. Fat is a great flavor carrier, so developing techniques to replace this characteristic is key. Students are taught to rely on the carmelization of food and other techniques to create a wonderful flavor. Fast cooking/grilling and the development of flavors through carmelization of the protein in food are critical.

* Coping with a fickle public. We may say we want nutrition but then we order old-style desserts. Chefs need to offer foods that satisfy both desires.

NUTRITIONAL PROFILE COMPARISON

Per serving	Nutrient Rich	Old Style
calories	216	386
fat (g)	6	15
saturated fat (g)	1	9
carbohydrates (g)	41	63
fiber (g)	4	3
sodium (mg)	72	208

* Finding fresh food. Food has to be fresh to be flavorful. Chefs are paying more attention to the food coming in the door. The chef who gets the best quality fresh food will get the best end result. Not a lot has to be done to these foods to make them taste great.

* Responding to a resurgence desire for comfort foods. Chefs will become better cooks as they are challenged to make these classic foods nutritious and delicious!

For further information on this topic contact: www.ciachef.edu and read the book, *The Professional Chef's Techniques for Healthy Cooking*.

he Basics

Yogurt Cheese

*S*ometimes it only takes one small step to begin a whole new attitude toward a future of promise, rather than the inevitability of pain!

I know that Treena and I are growing older and that this physical life will wind down, but that is no reason to stop looking for benefits by adopting small changes to match the aging process.

We really do eat a <u>little</u> less <u>every</u> year and try to move a <u>little</u> more. We actually plan to do so because energy is so absolutely precious. It is <u>the</u> resource needed for a happy retirement.

The Basics

Yogurt Cheese

I'm loath to overstate any one food or idea. However, the consistent use of 'yogurt cheese' instead of butter or margarine or cream has made a huge difference in our consumption of calories from fat. In our case, the actual savings over one year amounts to just over 40,000 or over 11 pounds of body fat — just with one food.

1. Find a 32-ounce tub of plain, nonfat yogurt that contains *no* thickeners, such as gelatin or starch (just check the ingredients). Don't get a yogurt with cornstarch or thickeners which stop the yogurt from separating. I've found that Dannon does one that's almost always readily available.

2 The method is so simple — it only takes 28 seconds! Use a yogurt strainer or a colander with absorbent kitchen toweling. Turn the yogurt into the strainer and place in the refrigerator for at least 8 hours or overnight: 50% of the whey drains away and you are left with yogurt cheese. The conversion to cheese (straining off the whey) takes about 12 hours. The 'cheese' becomes quite firm and the small lumps disappear, which makes it ideal for use in sauces. You don't have to worry about it or watch it. I've once left it for a week without a problem.

3 Add a soft tub light margarine (with no trans fatty acids) in equal proportions to create a cup of spread (you can also use 2/3 strained yogurt and 1/3 margarine proportion for even less fat and calories).

4. Other ways to use yogurt cheese:

* mix with maple syrup to serve alongside a slice of pie

* substitute for sour cream with baked potato, adding fresh ground pepper and chives

* serve as a sauce with poached chicken, using the yogurt cheese and chicken stock thickened with cornstarch and garnished with capers and pimento and a dash of parsley on the top

So, that's the decision. Can you take the time to shop for it and wait for it? Remember, it's a saving of at least 40,000 calories from fat — and it's *delicious!*

NUTRITIONAL PROFILE COMPARISON

Per 1/2 cup serving	Nutrient Rich
calories	127
fat (g)	0
saturated fat (g)	0
carbohydrates (g)	0
fiber (g)	0
sodium (mg)	174

Basic Pie Crust

Not only is this pie crust recipe reliable, it is relatively easy to prepare, with about 30 fewer calories than the old style recipe. Here's a helpful hint for preventing your rolled out dough from falling to pieces as you transfer it from the rolling sheet to the pie. Fold the dough that has been rolled out into half and then over again so that it is quartered. You can now pick it up easily. Place on top of the pie and then unfold completely to cover.

1. Combine the flour, sugar and salt in a food processor. Pour in the oil and pulse until mixed. Cut the margarine or butter into small pieces and add to the flour mixture. Pulse 10 times or until the mixture is full of lumps the size of small peas.

2. Pour in the vinegar and ice water. Pulse 10 more times or until the dough begins to hold together. Gather into 2 equal balls, wrap separately and refrigerate at least 30 minutes before rolling out.

3. This dough can, of course, be made by hand. Combine the flour, sugar and salt and stir in the oil. Add the margarine or butter and mix with a pastry cutter or 2 knives until the size of small peas. Add the vinegar and ice water and mix with a fork just until it starts to hold together. Gather into 2 balls, wrap and refrigerate as above.

Makes 2 crusts for 9" pies, 16 servings of a single crust pie.

Ingredients:

1 1/2 cups cake flour
1 teaspoon sugar
1/8 teaspoon salt
2 tablespoons non-aromatic olive oil
1/4 cup hard margarine or butter, frozen for 15 minutes (butter may be better)
1 teaspoon vinegar
4 tablespoons ice water

NUTRITIONAL PROFILE COMPARISON

Per serving	Nutrient Rich	Old Style
calories	78	107
fat (g)	5	6
saturated fat (g)	1	3
carbohydrates (g)	8	12
fiber (g)	0	0
sodium (mg)	52	177

Ingredients:

Basic Beef Stock

1 pound beef bones, fat trimmed off
1 teaspoon non-aromatic olive oil
1 onion, coarsely chopped
1/2 cup coarsely chopped leaves and tops of celery
1 cup coarsely chopped carrots
1 bay leaf
1 teaspoon dried thyme
6 black peppercorns
2 whole cloves
5 cups water

Basic Chicken, Turkey, or Duck Stock

1 teaspoon non-aromatic olive oil
1 onion, peeled and chopped
1/2 cup coarsely chopped celery tops
1 cup coarsely chopped carrots
carcass from a whole bird and any meat, fat, or skin scraps
1 bay leaf
2 sprigs fresh thyme or 1 teaspoon dried thyme
2 springs fresh parsley
6 black peppercorns
2 whole cloves
8 cups water

Basic Fish or Shrimp Stock

1 teaspoon non-aromatic olive oil
1 onion, peeled and chopped
1/2 cup coarsely chopped celery tops
2 sprigs fresh thyme or 1 teaspoon dried thyme
1 bay leaf
1 pound fish bones (no heads) or shrimp shells
6 black peppercorns
2 whole cloves
5 cups water

Stocks

Basic Beef Stock

1. Preheat the oven to 375°F (190°C). Place the beef bones in a roasting pan and cook until nicely browned, about 25 minutes. The browning produces a richer flavor and deeper color in the final stock.

2. Pour the oil into a large stockpot over medium heat. Add the onion, celery, and carrots and fry to release the volatile oils, 5 minutes. Add the bones, bay leaf, thyme, peppercorns, and cloves. Pour in the water, bring to a boil, reduce the heat and simmer 4 to 8 hours, adding more water if necessary. Skim off any foam as it rises to the surface.

3. Pour through a fine strainer, discard the solids, and skim off all the fat. The stock can be frozen for up to 6 months.

Makes 4 cups

Basic Chicken, Turkey, or Duck Stock

1. Pour the oil into a large stockpot over medium heat. Add the onion, celery tops, and carrots, and fry to release their volatile oils, 5 minutes. Add the carcass and seasonings and cover with 8 cups of water. Bring to a boil, reduce the heat, and simmer 2 to 4 hours, adding water if needed. Skim off any foam that rises to the surface.

2. Pour through a fine strainer, discard the solids, and skim off all the fat. The stock can be frozen for up to 6 months.

Makes 4 cups

Basic Fish or Shrimp Stock

1. Pour the oil into a large saucepan and saute the onion, celery tops, thyme, and bay leaf until onion is translucent, about 5 minutes. To ensure a light colored stock, be careful not to brown.

2. Add the fresh bones or shrimp shells, peppercorns, and cloves, cover the 5 cups water, bring to a boil, reduce the heat and simmer for 25 minutes.

3. Strain through a fine-mesh sieve and cheesecloth.

Makes 4 cups

Basic Vegetable Stock

1. Pour the oil into a large stockpot over medium heat, add the onion and garlic, and saute for 5 minutes. Add the rest of the ingredients and cover with 5 cups water.

2. Bring to a boil, reduce the heat, and simmer 30 minutes.

3. Strain through a fine-mesh sieve and cheesecloth.

Makes 4 cups

Basic Lamb Stock

1. Heat the oil in a chef's pan or deep skillet. Toss in the trim and stir to brown 1 or 2 minutes. Add the onion, garlic, and rosemary, stirring until the ingredients start to brown. Pour in the water, bring to a boil, reduce the heat and simmer while you prepare the rest of the stew. You will get a lot of flavor in just 15 or 20 minutes. Strain into a fat separator and pour 3 cups into the stew.

2. You can make more by returning the stock ingredients to the pan and adding 4 cups more water. Simmer another 20 minutes, de-fat and freeze for another time.

Bouquet Garni

1 bay leaf
2 sprigs fresh thyme or 1 teaspoon dried
6 peppercorns
2 whole cloves
3 sprigs parsley

Tie all the ingredients in a square of cheesecloth and use to flavor soups and stews.

Stock Separator/ De-fatting Cup

Ingredients:

Basic Vegetable Stock
1 teaspoon non-aromatic olive oil
1 onion, peeled and chopped
2 cloves garlic, peeled and bashed
1/2 teaspoon freshly grated ginger root
1/2 cup coarsely chopped carrot
1 cup coarsely chopped celery
1 cup coarsely chopped turnip
1/4 cup coarsely chopped leeks, white and
   light green parts only
3 sprigs fresh parsley
1/2 teaspoon black peppercorns
5 cups water

Basic Lamb Stock
1 teaspoon non-aromatic olive oil
trim from the lamb steaks
1/2 large onion, roughly chopped
2 cloves garlic, bashed and chopped
3" (8 cm) sprig rosemary
4 cups water

Techniques and Tools

Arrowroot Slurry

Try using arrowroot flour, rather than gluten flours or corn starch, to thicken sauces and stews. Arrowroot does not need to boil to thicken and adds no flavor or color to the sauce.

Spurtle

Try using this bamboo utensil for stirring food in use in non-stick pans. Spurtles come in a variety of shapes, some even with holes or slots for easy stirring and beating, some with straight edges for scraping or de-glazing pans.

Stock Separator/De-Fatting Cup

Use this utensil to 'de-fat' liquids for sauces and stocks. This utensil is a large measuring cup with a spout that comes out the bottom. Fat rises to the top and the 'de-fatted' liquid can be poured out for the sauce or stock, leaving the fat behind.

Roll Cutting

This is an Asian technique for cutting long round vegetables like carrots into different shapes than the standard plain or diagonal slice. Roll the vegetable around just a half of a roll at a time and cut through it to get a different look and texture.